50 EASTERN IDAHO HIKING TRAILS
(and Trouting Retreats)

50 EASTERN IDAHO HIKING TRAILS
(and Trouting Retreats)

The Sawtooth, White Cloud, Boulder, Smoky, Pioneer, Big Horn Crags, Lemhi and Teton Ranges

By Ron Mitchell

Library of Congress Catalog Card No. 79-65581

ISBN: 0-87108-551-8

First Edition
1 2 3 4 5 6 7 8 9

Printed in the United States of America

ACKNOWLEDGEMENTS

I wish to express my gratitude to Don Lowe and Oral Bullard for their technical assistance in preparing this manuscript, and my especial thanks to Nick Bielemeier of Columbia Photo in Hood River, Oregon, without whose logistical support I couldn't have done this book.

INTRODUCTION

The journals of Lewis and Clark are almost electric with exclamations of excitement and awe. And nowhere on their epic journey to the Pacific did the land provoke more superlatives than when they reached what is now eastern Idaho. After relatively easy going through the wide valleys of western Montana, they suddenly were confronted by a high wall of snow-capped mountains (the Bitterroots) at whose height Lewis marvelled. The explorers detoured south searching for a way around them, crossing into Idaho's Lemhi Valley, only to discover that the huge mountains multiplied into a foot-travelers nightmare of endless jagged ranges extending to the horizon and probably beyond.

But there was a river (the Salmon, famed River of No Return) that had, the Indians told them, gouged a path through the mountains. A short reconnaisance of the Salmon's raging white-water told Lewis and Clark they couldn't hitch a ride on her back in canoes. Stymied but undaunted, they decided to find another route to Oregon. Sure, if they had months to spare and an assured supply of food they might eventually pick their way through those mountains, but they didn't.

And what Lewis and Clark couldn't do this book is designed to help modern backpackers *do:* to explore those same seemingly endless mountain ranges of eastern Idaho that in places are as wild as when they defeated Thomas Jefferson's favorite explorers. It is a vast chunk of Rocky Mountain terrain, larger than the states of Delaware, Connecticut, Hawaii, Rhode Island, and New Hampshire combined. Fourteen separate ranges between ten and twelve thousand feet rear from arid valleys, varying in type from the pyramidal structure of the sedimentary-conglomerate fault block ranges along the Idaho-Montana-Wyoming border to the granitic sawtoothed crags of the Salmon River country, carved by wind, water, and frost from the Idaho Batholith—the largest extrusion of granite rock in the country. Foliage varies from verdant, moist douglas fir forests of the meadow-splotched western Tetons to thin stands of Englemann spruce edging fragile, tiny parks of sagebrush and grass of the arid Lost River and Lemhi Ranges.

The area is a veritable cornucopia of spectacular hiking trails, and in compiling this book the problem wasn't in finding suitable trails but in choosing between equally stunning vistas. Rather than an inclusive catalogue of the region's trails, this book should be considered an introductory sampling. The author has included a variety of trail types to satisfy everyone's topographical sweet tooth: trails in valleys, on ridges, to mountain summits, and to lakes. Although most offer sweeping views, some are reminiscent of the densely wooded, close country of northern Maine. All lead into true wilderness country, and can be extended into longer loop trips via connecting trails or cross-country routes. Though off-trail hiking usually is impossible in the rain-drenched and consequently brush-choked Cascades, it's commonly done in the drier Rockies to escape the trail-hugging crowds and find solitude, and for sheer adventure.

BACKPACKING THE IDAHO ROCKIES

Books abound on backpacking equipment and techniques, but a brief introduction to eastern Idaho might start the parties concerned off on more comfortable footing.

Weather can be the bane or blessing of wilderness outings, and in the northern Rockies it follows a distinct cycle, of rain piddling out in May, scorching 90-degree days with blue skies through June and July, with late afternoon thunderstorms prevalent in August. September comes in sunny and cool, then in its third week feigns winter, complete with snow that evaporates under high, blue, windswept skies of October's Indian summer. Sounds manageable.

But because of extremes in elevation of from 6,000 to almost 13,000 feet, incredibly abrupt weather changes occur that can prove lethal. In August 1976 at Kane Lake it snowed two days, piling up 11 inches deep at 10,000 feet. I met a couple from Vermont retreating down the trail who were safely bundled in woolens thanks to foresight. Prolonged exposure to rain and wind at 8,000 feet where I've measured the windchill factor at 26 degrees in July can, and does, kill people. Always carry a windbreaker, a felt or wool hat, a rain-proof garment, and a wool sweater. I've seldom used a flashlight on one-day trips, but when I did I needed it badly. A first-aid kit is essential for longer trips. Knives can be worth their weight in platinum, and I've never carried water. Even in '77's drought drinking water was always available along the trail.

Certain cussed critters in Idaho's crags can cause you consternation, namely mosquitoes and ticks, in that order. The epicenter, so to speak, of mosquito abundance climbs in elevation as summer progresses, following the edge of melting snow upward. By August they'll have died out below 7,000 feet, be abundant at 8,000, and be downright virulent at 9,000. If season and elevation predict skeeters at your planned destination, there are 4 combatants you can enlist: a thick wool shirt and levis, a bee keeper-type headnet, spray, and a tent with mosquito netting. I carry a 6-ounce stick of roll-on repellent for the backs of my hands, use clothing to protect my body, and a headnet to shield my face since I dislike spraying it, and since spray becomes diluted and ineffective from perspiration.

In 19 years of hiking in Idaho I've seen no rattlesnakes above 6,500 feet, although I've met them at 6,000 along the Little Wood River. But ticks—now there is a real boogey bug. Some Idaho wood ticks carry Rocky Mountain Spotted Fever. They're mostly a threat in June; however, I picked two off my thigh this last September. Their bite transmits to the blood a micro organism (*Rickettsia rickettsii*) which produces in 5 to 7 days symptoms of weakness, chills, nausea, vomiting and headache. Unfortunately these symptoms duplicate those for the benign affliction of altitude sickness. More exclusively, spotted fever symptoms are bloodshot eyes, eye sensitivity to light, sore eyeballs, and a deep, dusky flush on the face. Between the third and fifth days after the onset of symptoms the spots appear. To avoid this nasty situation, investigate any crawling sensation, and check your skin at night and your clothes at dawn before donning them. If bitten, pull the tick out with a slow, steady pull if he's just started chomping, or if he's in deep, coat him with turpentine and wait a couple hours for him to back out. Inoculations against spotted fever are available, but your chances of being bitten are slight; and antibiotics have rendered it non-lethal.

Etiquette, the lubricant of social interaction, is important in the woods, where the code of behavior of backpackers directly affects the degree of enjoyment other hikers experience. Hiking with a newcomer to wilderness last summer, I had some difficulty convincing her that the tiny gum wrappers she persisted in dropping really were a blight to the landscape because they were unnatural. Please don't mimic her; *any* litter, large or small, is out-of-place as a nun cursing, especially away from the trail where one least expects it. So pack out all unburnables. Burn used toilet paper on the spot and, with a child's toy sand shovel that weighs nothing bury fecal material 5 inches deep in topsoil where bacterial action will render it soil in a week. Regarding campsites, Rangers in the Sawtooth Wilderness Area lamented that their two biggest use-impact problems are fire rings and trenching. So please, use existing rings of fire-blackened stones instead of building your own (or better yet carry a small gas stove), and don't dig trenches around your tent to trap rainwater. Thanks, we're in this together.

FISHING ALPINE LAKES

High lakes in the Rockies more often than not support populations of trout—originally stocked hatchery fish, true; but after years in natural habitats they are wild fish. Some lakes provide excellent angling, but they shouldn't be depended on as a source of protein for extended trips; the trout may not be biting, and it would be unsporting to kill more than a brace of fish from a non or marginally reproducing population. The Idaho Fish and Game Dept. no longer stocks lakes lacking natural reproduction every other year because of a shortage of funds, and hikers killing limits of trout quickly decimates the population, reducing angling quality for all. Please limit your catch and not vice versa, except in lakes where trout are obviously outstripping the food supply. An exception to this rule are brook trout, which spawn in lakes and quickly overpopulate unless checked by angling pressure.

As yet there are no definitive works dealing specifically with alpine lake fishing. Although *Trout Fishing for Backpackers* by Ron Cordes, and *Fishing the High Country,* by Trey Combs, represent fine beginnings, this is still a relatively unscrutinized sphere of the angling world. Space limits an in-depth study here, but for hikers who have never angled lakes at 8,000 feet, some generalizations may help.

First, pack a flyrod with both sinking and floating lines, or a spinning rod with a plastic bubble, and fish with flies, not salmon eggs, worms, or minnow-duplicating spinners, none of which occur in high lakes. Use smaller flies than at lower elevations because insects are smaller up high, mostly sizes 12 to 24. Patterns are available from fly fishing specialty shops and should include midge pupal and adult copies in olive, gray, black, brown, and ruby from size 16 to 24; fur-bodied nymphs in black, dark brown, tan, olive, and gray size 12 to 18; standard dry flies with bodies of gray, dark brown, white, and pale olive in 12's and 16's; caddis dries and pupae in brown, tan, black, yellowish orange, and olive in sizes 10 to 20; size 14 and 22 reddish brown alpine ant and a size 10 in black; damselfly nymphs in pale olive and gray size 10 2X long. Fat, size 8 dragonfly nymphs in gray and dark olive complete the selection.

Finding trout in lakes means fishing the shallows, where sunlight penetrates and fosters food forms, although the depths are sometimes productive. Areas near out- and inlets, and reefs are prime feeding grounds. From late June to early July trout feed in the afternoon, and as the water warms with the season's progression they feed earlier and later each day until cooler weather in late September reverses the process. When water reaches 63 degrees in brook trout lakes they tend to feed only in the evening. However, above 9000 feet trout often feed all day on sporadically hatching *Chironomidae* midges. Good Luck. Shoulda been here yesterday.

HOW TO USE THIS BOOK

Preceding the text for each trail is a list of 6 important facts:

Hiking **distance** is measured one way, and mileages often conflict with those on signposts because trails are rerouted or the Forest Service used incorrect map mileages rather than the actual distance walked.

Elevation gain and loss are listed to enable the reader to quickly compute a hike's steepness relative to the distance travelled. After hiking and comparing the steepness and distance factors of a few hikes in this book you'll be able to compare them with a prospective trail's and have a good idea how tough the hike will be.

By comparing the **high point** for a trail with the last trail's or the one to which you are acclimated you will know if its higher (or lower) elevation requires allowing additional time.

Hiking time calculations, and even caloric requirements charts, which can't allow for wide divergence in individual metabolic rates, involve some subjective evaluations. Hikers comparing their pace with that of a measuring device is as good as any method. For this book the device was a 150-pound 28-year-old male acclimated to 7,000 feet and walking at a leisurely pace that averaged 1.8 miles per hour over 5 months.

Periods when trails are **open** vary yearly depending on snowpack and subsequent spring weather. If you're planning a trip in June or October it's wise to contact one of the national forest headquarters where you'll be hiking.

Topographical map information is included to not only prove such a wonderful place really exists, but also to assist you in purchasing adjoining maps necessary to make the loop and cross-country hikes suggested but not shown on the text's maps. Stores outside Idaho won't carry them, but you can order them. Visit the nearest office or nautical supply store carrying topographical maps and ask to see a key map for Idaho, or write the U.S. Geological Survey, Federal Center, Denver, Colorado 80225. Then correlate the map in this book with the key map and select the necessary adjacent maps, then order them from the U.S.G.S. or through the store. Incidentally, *Jensen and Graves* in Boise stocks all Idaho topos, and *Snug Company* in Ketchum carries some.

The text for each trail is in 3 parts: The first describes the scenic features, probable wildlife, and possible loop trips. The second gives access directions. All roads to the trailheads were negotiated in a VW Bug, and it is noted when they are marginal for low-slung modern autos. The final part includes, in addition to crucial on-trail directions, a description of the trail as you would see it as you hiked along. Coupling it with the accompanying photo(s) allows you to ascertain a trail's scenic character beforehand and thereby choose a hike suiting your fancy. Location of campsites, water stops, and fishing suggestions are included.

The accompanying maps are enlarged or reduced sections of U.S. Geological Survey topographical maps, which are quite, but not absolutely accurate. The author walked each of the trails in the text in '76-'77, and has made corrections where there were trail-location errors or changes. Even the faintest trails in this book can easily be hiked by correlating the text description with the map; but knowing how to interpret the squiggly lines on the maps is essential to hassle-free cross-country travel. Libraries are rife with books especially devoted to the topic, but a few basics here will suffice for anyone who hasn't read one.

Those parallel lines are called contour lines, and they connect points of equal elevation, and are spaced either 40 or 80 feet apart. Their distance apart signifies steepness of the terrain; very close means very steep and far apart means flatter. Where they curve in towards a creek, it is a gulley, and lines coming to points signify ridges. Circles growing steadily smaller are peaks. On your first day hiking with this book stop at a prominent landmark, and compare it with the lines on the map, and you'll see a skeleton-on-paper of the real thing! By comparing and visualizing for a couple of hours at various points you'll be able to plot a practical, safe cross-country course. Besides avoiding cliffs and utilizing passes, remember that timber and brush may be obstacles, and while appearing on the original maps as shades of green, on the book's black and white copies they appear as shades of gray.

Contents

LEGEND

⬢	Starting Point
– · – · – · –	Trail Described in Text
– – – – –	Incorrect or Alternate Trail
· · · · · · · · ·	Faint Trail or Suggested Route
▲	Campsite
✖	Viewpoint
■	Building
8.0	Mileage
227	Trail or Road No.
===	Access Road
– – ✖ – –	Bridge

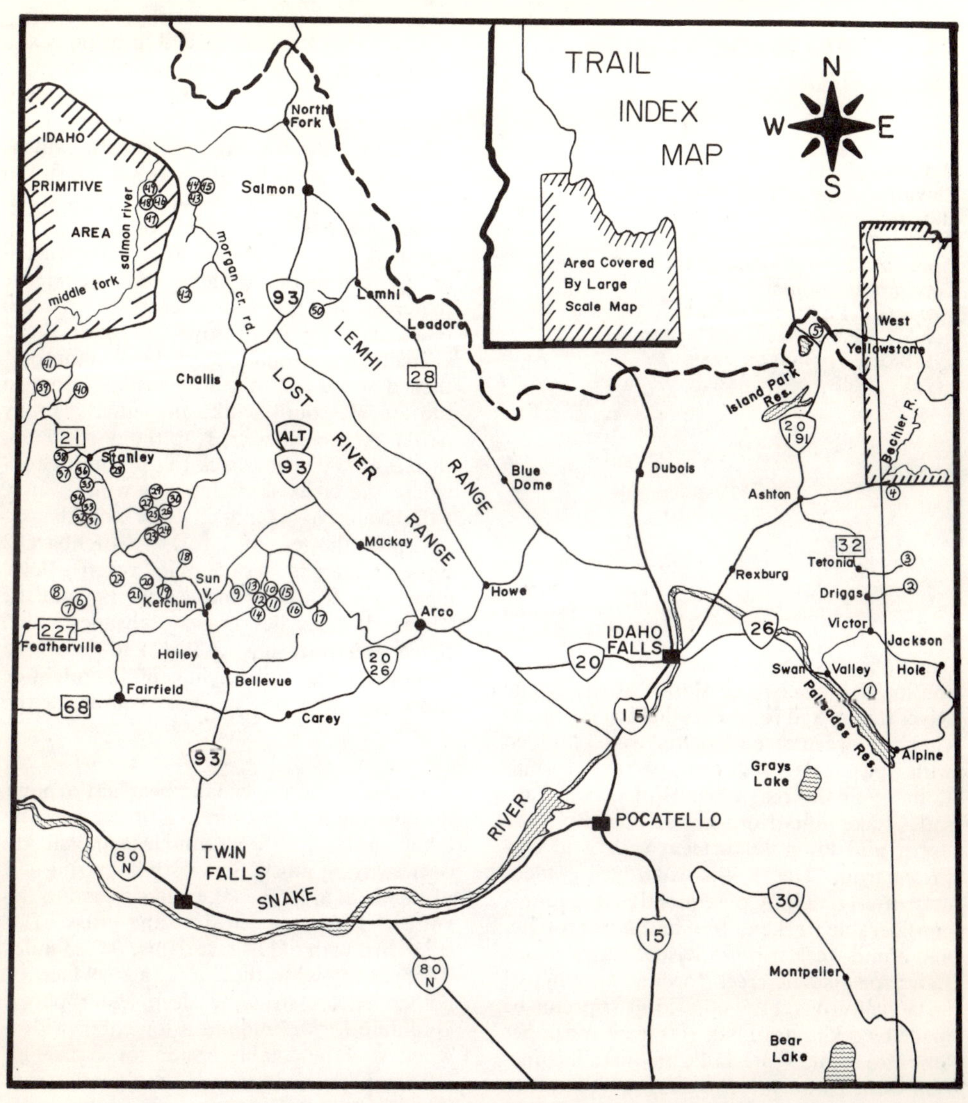

TRAIL
INDEX
MAP
N
W
E
S
IDAHO
PRIMITIVE
AREA
middle fork salmon river
North Fork
Salmon
morgan cr. rd.
Area Covered
By Large
Scale Map
West
Yellowstone
Bechler R.
Lemhi
Leadore
LEMHI
RANGE
93
Challis
LOST
RIVER
RANGE
ALT
93
Stanley
Blue
Dome
Dubois
Island Park
Res.
Ashton
Mackay
Sun
V.
Ketchum
Hailey
Bellevue
Carey
Fairfield
Featherville
227
68
93
Arco
Howe
20
26
20
15
IDAHO
FALLS
Rexburg
Tetonia
Driggs
Victor
Jackson
Hole
Swan Valley
Palisades Res.
Alpine
26
32
Grays
Lake
POCATELLO
TWIN
FALLS
SNAKE
RIVER
80
N
80
N
15
30
Montpelier
Bear
Lake
21
28

1 PALISADES CREEK TRAIL

Distance: 7.5 miles
Elevation gain: 1,070 feet
High point: 6,640 feet
Allow 4 to 5 hours
Open late June through October
Topographic maps:
  U.S.G.S. Palisades Peak
  7.5′   1966
  U.S.G.S. Thompson Peak
  7.5′   1966

The Palisades Creek Trail No. 084 begins on the lower pine-covered slopes of the Snake River Range and follows rollicking Palisades Creek between steep canyon walls studded with spectacular sedimentary rock formations to finally reach beautiful Upper Palisades Lake in its fiord-like setting. Both the upper and lower lakes teem with wild cutthroat trout. The trail is wide, well-graded, and utterly safe. Consequently, it endures considerable weekend foot and horse traffic, and a mid-week trip is advised. Carry tennis shoes for a single creek-fording. In August, an adventurous 11.5 mile loop trip can be made by taking trail No. 100 from the upper lake into scenic Waterfall Canyon to its junction with trail No. 102 atop a 9,600-foot saddle, and down Lake Canyon to Lower Palisades Lake.

Drive on U.S. 26 from Palisades Reservoir to the town of Palisades, then 2.1 miles north to the sign at the junction of road No. 254 indicating Palisades Creek Campground, and turn right. At about 0.2 mile the gravel road forks right and left, but take the third, middle fork. At another fork go right, and 200 feet ahead take a left at a fork. At 1.5 miles take the middle of 3 forks and continue 0.6 miles to the campground and drive its loop to the sign at its east end indicating the Palisades Creek Trail.

Climb gently paralleling the creek through dappled shade of cottonwoods, pines, and junipers. Rock bluffs eroded into spires and monuments jut from both sides of looming canyon walls. Syringa, fleabane, dogwood, Indian paintbrush and lupine splash the trailside slopes. At 1.3 miles the canyon widens at a bridge, and the valley ahead appears to end in a huge amphitheatre. Climb moderately away from the creek for .5 mile, then rejoin it 200 feet above. Watch for ruffed grouse feeding on huckleberries. Again leave the creek and rejoin at stream level. At 2.0 miles the canyon narrows as you make 2 switchbacks around a rock promontory, then descend 0.7 mile to a bridge, cross to the creek's south bank, and enter a rocky defile. At 3.8 miles cross to the north bank, then 0.4 mile ahead back to the south bank, where the creek is a chute of white water. Climb gently, making 2 steep switchbacks, and take the left of 3 forks. Switchback 2 more times and at 4.5 miles reach a level clearing with tables and a grill. Beyond the screen of trees lies Lower Palisades Lake. Since deer mice pose a threat to food and equipment here, overnight camping might be more enjoyable on the grassy flat beside the lake's inlet.

To reach the upper lake bear left around the clearing and descend to a bridge over the lake's outlet that flows gin-clear and slickly over swaying moss. Beavers inhabit this end of the lake. Skirt the lake and descend to the valley floor, a willow-and-grass flat splotched with old beaver dams. At 5.5 miles it narrows, with the creek a necklace of golden riffles stringing deep azure pools. Undulate for 0.5 mile to a log cabin with a wood stove and table beside the creek—an excellent spot for lunch. Climb gently from the creek through open woods for 0.2 mile, traverse 150 feet above the creek, and at 6.8 miles go right at a fork and descend to the creek, ignoring the log spanning the creek and crossing safely by wading the shallows in tennis shoes. Enter a grove of firs and at the sign separating horse and foot trails bear right. Make six steep switchbacks, passing a sign noting Palisades Creek gushing from the natural wall damming the lake, and wind gently through lodgepoles and firs to reach the lake at 7.5 miles. Flat, shaded campsites lie to your right across the outlet or at the lake's head along the inlet. Trout fishing is excellent in the lake's numerous coves and by the in- and outlets.

Lower Palisade Lake

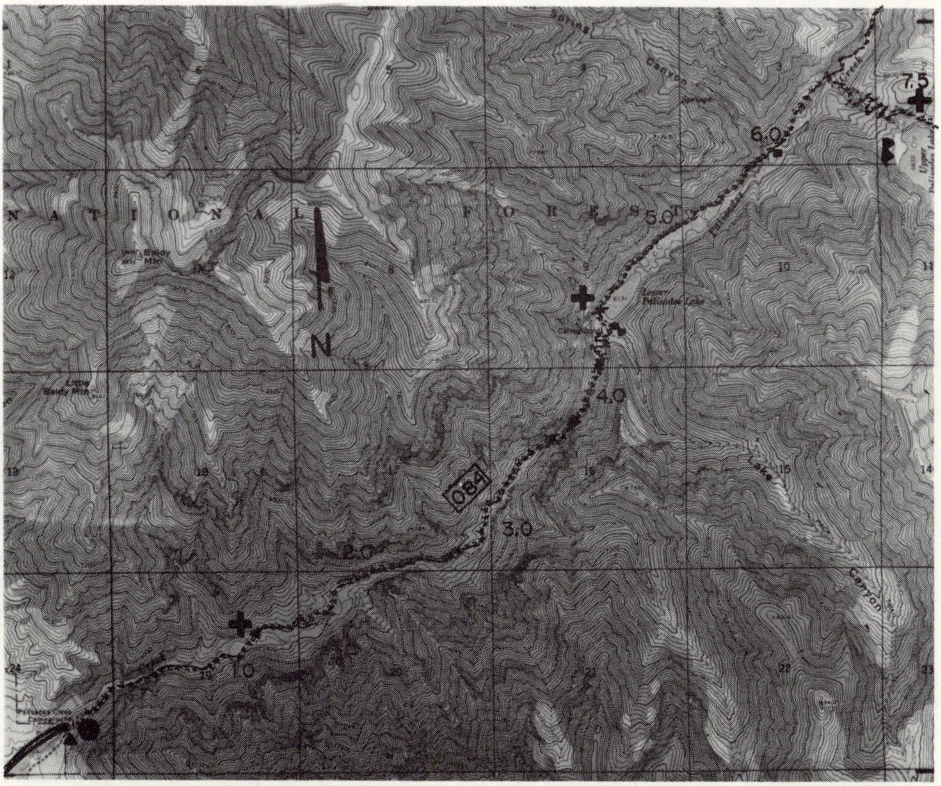

2 TABLE MOUNTAIN

Distance: 6.3 miles
Elevation gain: 4,145 feet
High point: 11,101 feet
Allow 6 hours
Open July to early October
Topographic maps:
   U.S.G.S. Granite Basin, Wyo.
   7.5′   1968
   U.S.G.S. Grand Teton, Wyo.
   7.5′   1968

From the summit of 11,101-foot Table Mountain a hiker has the rare view of the west face of the Grant Teton, and the jagged heart of the Teton Range north and south. To the east, Jackson Hole is visible 4,000 feet below, while west the forgotten "Idaho" side of the Tetons unfolds. Unlike the sheer eastern face, this western side slopes in long U-shaped glacial valleys walled with sedimentary rock cliffs separating stair-step terraced meadows.

Though the trail is only 6.3 miles, 6 hours is recommended because of the steady incline at high altitude. Campsites abound along the first 4 miles. The treeless alpine terrain south of Table Mountain offers unlimited cross-country travel; or one can intersect the trail down to Solitude Lake and Cascade Canyon to Jackson Hole; or go south and make a loop to Alaska Basin and down trail No. 024 along the South Fork Teton Creek to Teton Creek Campground.

From the sign in downtown Driggs, Idaho, drive the road to Grand Targhee Resort to a fork and turn left to Alta, reach another fork and sign stating Treasure Mountain Camp and Teton Canyon right on road No. 009, and drive about 4.8 miles past Teton Creek Campground on the right to the road's end, where a sign on the left marks the North Fork Teton Creek Trail.

Unlike beaten paths of the Jackson Hole side, this trail is a narrow trace. At a fork a few feet from the sign go left between 2 blazed trees and climb in 4 switchbacks through dense aspens underpinned with scarlet paintbrush and lupine, then climb steeply straight uphill, paralleling the North Fork out of sight but roaring. Through trees on the right glimpse glaciated peaks above the South Fork's canyon. At 0.5 mile level out into parkland studded with granite boulders. The valley's right side is solid conifers, while the left is slim-trunked, fluttery-leafed aspens hedged by prim stands of spruce and fir. Climb gently another half mile, then moderately through clumps of bistort, cross the creek admist 8-foot willows, and reach a fork in a shaded glen. Bear left to a sign pointing to South Leigh Creek left, Table Mountain right. Ahead the valley widens almost a mile, with a serrated snowy headwall visible high in the distance. Climb gently through intermittent shade, leap a creek, cross the North Fork via logs at 2.5 miles, then climb erratically in the open through wildflowers and boulders. Ford the creek again, then again on a log, and at 3.2 miles reach an avalanche path of broken conifers. Wind uphill and into forest and cross the creek at the last sheltered campsite below timberline.

Proceed through a small clearing, make 4 steep switchbacks to a rock wall, then switchback twice more to a verdant basin purple with lupine and bluebells. Cross it at a steep grade to reach timberline at 4.0 miles, make steep switchbacks for another mile, and top out on a ridge edged with cornices. Turn left and reach a point where, looking west, you can see the vast dry expanse of the Snake River Plains, and to the south the Teton's western slope of rock walls and grassy benches splotched with snowfields. Fortunately, from here you can see Table Mountain, for a mile ahead the trail fades. Simply walk the bare ridge to the base of the table itself, aiming for the south-facing side and a rock cairn. Here the trail resurrects for 3 right, left, right switchbacks to the summit.

Grand Teton from Table Mountain

3 GREEN LAKE

Distance: 5.3 miles
Elevation gain: 2,060 feet; loss: 700 feet
High point: 9,080 feet
Allow 3 hours
Open late June to early October
Topographic map:
  U.S.G.S. Granite Basin, Wyoming
  7.5′   1968

The Green Lake Trail traverses an alpine splendor that I suspect was the location for the filming of *The Sound of Music*. Four-fifths of it climbs across tilted expanses of lush flowered meadow edged and seemingly decorated with proportioned stands of prim, spire-shaped spruce and fir. From the ridge one can see west across the wheat and grain fields of the Teton Basin, in September a sur-realistic checkerboard of yellow and choco-late brown, and beyond to the hazy blue rumor of the Lemhi Range. North one can see Montana's Madison Range, and east 11,000-foot summits of the Tetons jut up from mostly meadowed upper slopes. At trail's end four lakes hold cutthroat trout in rolling basins where elk and deer graze and bear tracks were rampant in '74 and '76.

This hike is tailor-made for a loop trip. From Green Lake you can hike south into Granite Basin, then down the S.F. Tin Cup Creek via the Andy Stone Trail, or go north on the Dry Ridge Trail, or down North Leigh Creek, both trails ending back at your car.

From Tetonia drive east on Idaho 33 about 3 miles, and where the road turns 90 degrees right continue straight ahead for 50 yards to an intersection and sign on the left directing you straight ahead to North and South Leigh Creeks 5 miles. Drive 2.8 miles to another sign on the left stating N. Leigh Cr. and turn left. Drive about 4 miles cross-ing Leigh Cr. twice, a good cutthroat and brook trout stream, and reach the Dry Ridge Trail sign on your left. Follow a grassy track 400 yards to a sign stating Green Mountain Trail Tin Cup Creek Green Lake 5. Drive right about 150 yards to a bare signpost and park under some trees.

From the signpost cross the creek, pausing to fill your canteen (no water on the trail), walk 70 yards and make 4 switchbacks to a ridge. Continue switchbacking erratically but never steeply across the timbered back of a ridge through a grass and brush under-story, at .8 mile catching a glimpse north of high, slanting meadows on Dry Ridge. Avoiding the blocked-off old road segments, finally rejoin the road just as it becomes a trail at 1.3 miles and follow it to a fork in a meadow. That sheer, flat-topped scarp about 2 miles away on your right and 1800 feet above you is Beard Mountain. Take the left fork for 150 yards and fork left again up 5 steep switchbacks through aspens to an-other park at 1.8 miles. This is an ideal spot for a photo of Beard Mountain from across rolling meadows with an 80-135 lens. Con-tinue climbing very steeply without switch-backs for .5 miles, then veer right to traverse a huge meadow studded with copses of firs on the right and the ridgetop a few yards up to the left. At 2.9 miles swing steeply left, then right and ease to a moderate traverse at 3.3 miles. Half-mile ahead reach a sign and descend left switchbacking into the meadows of North Leigh Creek and veer right along the base of Green Mountain's triple-tiered 800-foot cliff on your right. Cross a knoll and descend past a tarn to a fork at 4.9 and, bearing left, reach another fork and sign at 5.1 indicating Green Lake is left, Granite Basin right. Descend another .2 miles to Green Lake, deep, lined with tall conifers, with an irregular granite wall buttressing its far shore.

By following the lake's inlet you can reach 3 upper lakes. Best camping is in the trees east of the outlet, or at the upper lakes. Green Lake's native cutthroats reach 20'', but since growth is slow at this altitude and reproduction is skimpy, please return all large trout and limit your kill of smaller fish, which cruise the shallow bays along the north shore and feed heavily on midges all summer.

Cutthroat comes ashore at Green Lake

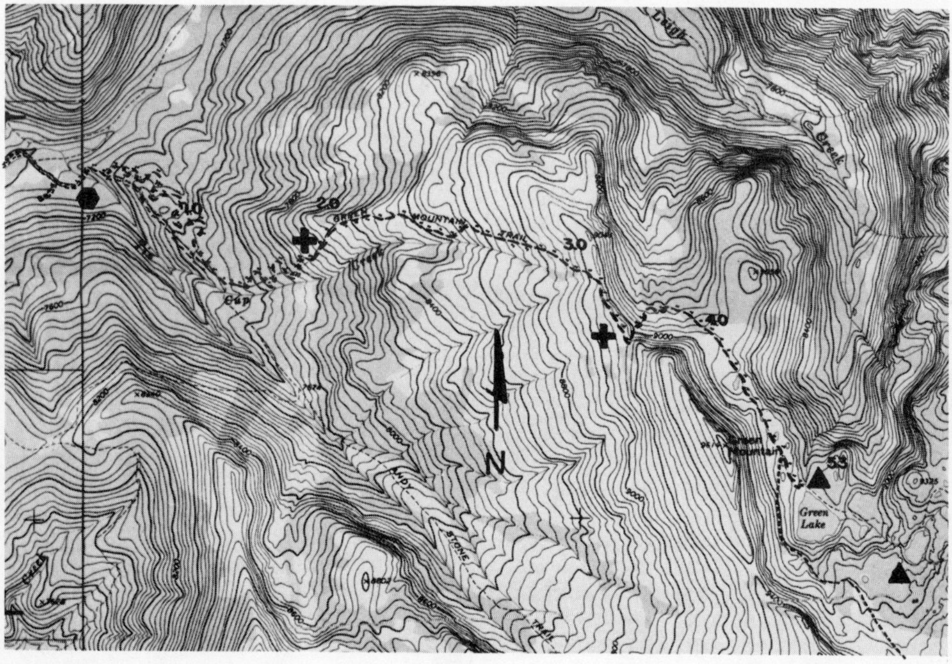

4 BECHLER RIVER

Distance: 4.7 miles
Elevation gain: 300 feet
High point: 6,420 feet
Allow 2 hours
Open mid-June to November
Topographic maps:
  U.S.G.S. Grassy Lake Res.
  15′ 1956
  U.S.G.S. Warm River Butte
  15′ 1957

Unlike Glacier, Yellowstone National Park isn't considered in the hiker's domain; travelogue posters depict hordes of tourists snapping Kodaks at bears and geysers or clinging awkwardly to saddlehorns astride slew-footed nags. But the park's wild southwest corner, dubbed the Cascade Corner because it holds more cataracts than the rest of the park combined, offers a network of gentle to moderate trails through meadow, bluff, and lodgepole country whose streams below waterfalls teem with trout that have never seen a hatchery. The trail along the Bechler, a classical western meadow stream in its upper reaches, begins at Cave Falls and passes Bechler Falls, both wide, low cataracts, and parallels the clear, cold, blue river most of the way. The river begins in cold pine-canyon springs and meanders through elk meadows, then makes a swift, riffling dash over blue-black bedrock to join the Fall River at Cave Falls. Other trails equally lovely follow Mountain Ash and Boundary Creeks, and a two-mile jaunt leads to Lilypad Lake from the fork to the Bechler Ranger Station. Elk and deer are frequently seen in summer, but the dreaded grizzlies are seldom encountered.

From Ashton, Idaho follow Idaho 47 east through Marysville to a fork, going left to Warm River, then in 3 miles right to Bechler Ranger Station and Cave Falls, about 18 miles. The road becomes gravel, then assumes pavement inside the park, ending at a turnaround at Cave Falls. Pick up the trail at the sign stating Bechler Falls Bechler River Trail at the east end of the turnaround.

Hike along the river, winding gently to moderately, with intermittent views of the river flowing slickly over its wide bed of blue-black rock that periodically turns to thin foaming riffles seemingly issuing from the rock in lines across the river. At 1.1 miles dip then climb steeply to a point overlooking Bechler Falls, a low, wide falls that plunges into a race of pocket water in a canyon where rainbows to 20″ lurk. Climb moderately past the falls where the river abruptly becomes a meandering meadow stream flowing slickly between grassy banks. Good fishing for small rainbows here, requiring a downstream cast. Wind along the river another 2.3 miles, then at a fork and sign stating Mountain Ash Creek right, go left, winding into lodgepole woods to another fork at 4.2 miles. Go right, and after .5 gentle miles reach the waist-high grass of Bechler Meadows at Boundary Creek.

Camping space and water is everywhere, and trails lead to Lilypad Lake, and farther up beside the Bechler to more waterfalls and on towards Madison Junction, or up Boundary Creek to Buffalo Lake. Best fishing lies an hour's hike up Boundary Creek, or about 2 miles up the main trail along the Bechler. Two forks of the Bechler meander through the meadow, but the best fishing is in the main river from the canyon downstream into the meadows. Blue-winged olive dries and nymphs are effective from July to August, when the grasshopper hatches begin. But green grass and immature hoppers persist into late August, meaning few actually fall into the stream even on windy days until early September, so be sure and stock ordinary nymphs and dries.

Fly casters in Bechler Meadows

Bechler Falls

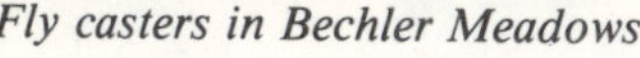

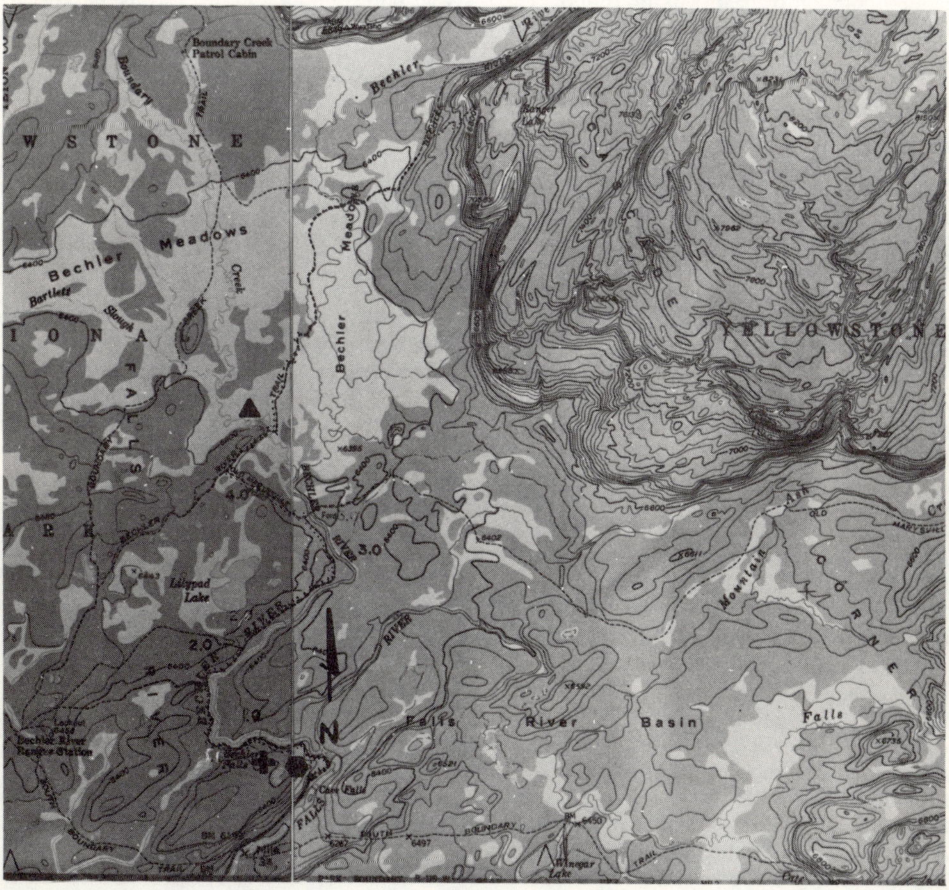

5 TARGHEE CREEK

Distance: 3.4 miles
Elevation gain: 1,750 feet
High point: 8,950 feet
Allow 2.5 hours
Open late June through October
Topographic maps:
  U.S.G.S. Targhee Pass
  7.5′   1964
  U.S.G.S. Targhee Peak
  7.5′   1964

Few people make this hike, one of the wildest and most beautiful in Idaho. The trail climbs beside limpid Targhee Creek—a prime spawning stream for Henry's Lake's cutthroats—into rolling alpine meadows above timberline dotted with lakes straddling the Continental Divide. There is room for miles of cross-country rambling up here, hidden basins to explore, peaks to scale. Moose are plentiful in the lower canyon, and elk and deer summer above timberline. From the ridge above Edwards Lake you can see north along the Divide, and northeast along the jagged crest of the Madison Range. Fishing in Targhee Creek closes July 1st, and none of the lakes hold trout. But anyone lusting to see abundant big game and a yen to explore could consume 4 days in Targhee Creek's headwaters.

Drive on U.S. 20-191 from Island Park east towards West Yellowstone. After passing the highway 287 turnoff left to Henry's Lake continue another 2.4 miles on 191 to the Howard Spring Wayside on the right. About 300 yards above the wayside take a dirt road branching left off the highway and drive this dirt track about 1.1 miles to a fork. If the sign is still standing it'll state Hwy 191 1 mile left, Targhee Cr. 1 mile right. Bear right, ignoring another left fork at 1.5 miles and continue on the jeep trail into the creek's canyon another 2.5 miles and ford the creek to its west bank. Park on the near side, wade the creek, and begin the trail 70 feet uphill at the sign, "Targhee Creek Trail."

Immediately pass through a rock defile and climb undulating erratically parallel to the creek showing intermittently through the trees. Cross several grassy glades between patches of thick timber, pausing at 0.7 miles for a gander across the narrow canyon at rust-colored cliffs. Watch for moose here. At 1 mile skirt a small meadow ablaze with yellow flowers above which you can see the wild crags far up Targhee Creek's West Fork, then at 1.3 miles climb steeply in 2 switchbacks out of the main canyon and into the East Fork's draw, skirting another meadow's right side. The trail is faint, but head straight for a gap in the trees. This narrow band of forest opens into a park in a narrow gorge with pale ocher cliffs rearing close on the right. Climb moderately until at 1.8 miles the trail fades. Bear left and cross to the creek's west bank, pick up the trail and parallel it another .9 mile, then switchback uphill left, cross 2 clearings, then 3 rivulets in timber, and reach at 3.2 miles a meadow below a headwall. Follow the faint trail straight through lush vegetation, watching for rock cairns marking it for .2 mile, then veer left straight uphill. The trail fades again, but a route marked by cairns climbs in 2 lazy switchbacks and enters whitebark pines. Angle right from these trees to the first lake, fed by a spring on its far side. Far prettier country and stunning vistas can now be reached by hiking cross-country up Targhee Creek, heading generally northwest, using the map on the opposite page.

Rolling meadow country of Targhee Creek headwaters

Upper Targhee Creek

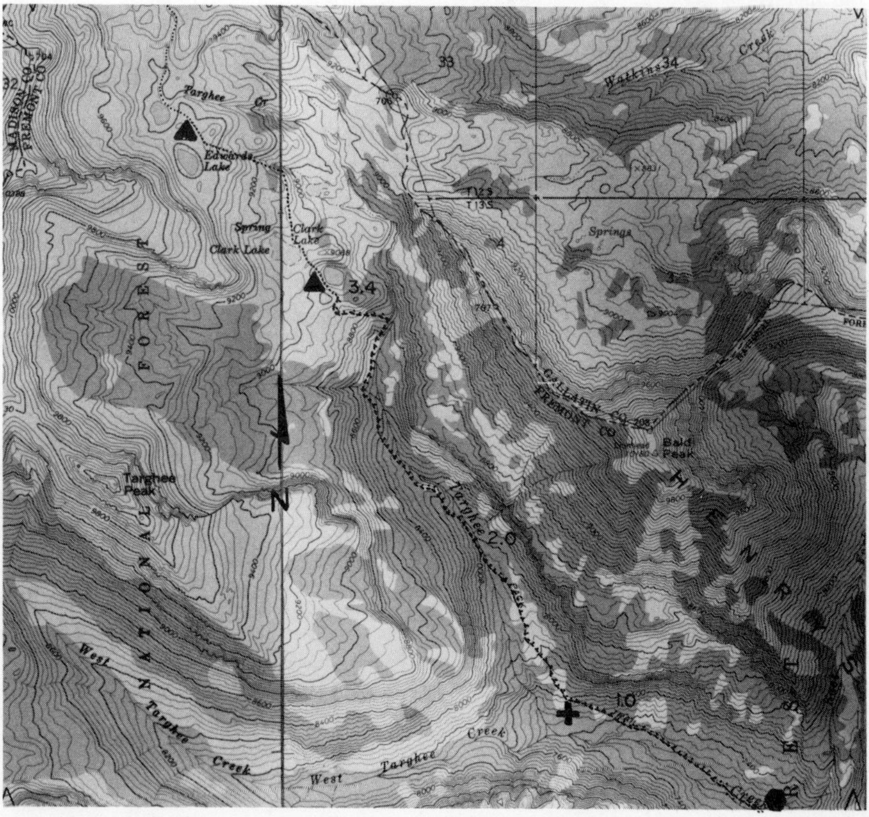

6 PERKONS LAKE

Distance: 3.2 miles
Elevation gain: 2,340 feet
High point: 8,800 feet
Allow 3 hours
Open July to mid-October
Topographic map:
  U.S.G.S. Marshall Peak
  7.5′   1964

The 10,000-foot peaks whose lakes and creeks form the headwaters of the South Fork Boise River are technically not part of the famous Sawtooth Range, even though they are simply across a creek called Ross Fork from the Sawtooth Range proper. Nevertheless, the one main ridge which holds all the lakes and alpine basins of the area matches them in height and scenic beauty. Major trails provide access, but because they are extremely steep and unpublicized they receive less traffic, keeping their upper extremities faint. But for the experienced outdoorsman who wants to loll in alpine scenery without crowds, this area is Shangri-la, with excellent trout fishing in 14 lakes, wildflowers galore, and mule deer and Rocky Mountain Goats plentiful.

Perkons Lake is a round, deep lake at the base of a 10,000-foot peak, and is reached by a short but steep trail, traversing several verdant hanging valleys rampant with wildflowers until the first frosts. Perkons supports a modest population of rainbow trout and receives some fishing pressure because its trail is the best in the area.

From Fairfield, situated on Idaho 68 between Mountain Home and Hailey, drive north on road 227 running down Fairview's main street, following all signs to Big Smoky Creek and its guard station. In about 32 miles reach Big Smoky Creek at a 3-way road fork, the right going to Big Smoky Guard Station, the left to the South Fork Boise River and Featherville. An alternate route to this same fork is to drive from Mountain Home to Featherville, then go east on road 227 for 23 miles. Either way, take the middle fork north (there was no sign

identifying this road in '77) over Fleck Summit and in about 12 well-graded miles reach another fork, the sign stating Bear Creek left. Keep right, crossing to the river's right bank, and in about 1.3 miles the road forks, the right going into trees, the left crossing Emma Creek. Both eventually rejoin; if you've a 4x4 go left, if a VW or similar high-clearance car, go right. In about 1½ miles where the forks join drive steeply up over a rough road impassable to passenger cars beyond a summit 2 miles on. Drive about 3.5 miles to Johnson Creek and ford it, and wind another very rough 3 miles through woods to a sign on the left stating Perkons Lake 3 miles. Turn left and follow the track 400 yards to the Ross Fork's lovely but fishless flow. Across the creek the ridge rises over 3,000 feet. Two forested ridges, like arms of a chair, descend on either side from the headwall that encircles Perkons Lake.

The trail begins as a gap in the brush on the south bank. Ford Ross Fork and scramble up the bank to this gap and in 300 feet intersect the Ross Fork Trail and a sign stating Perkons Lake straight ahead. Follow the trail towards the ridge across 250 yards of sage into tall woods, climbing erratically for .8 mile past clearings and log piles then climb steeply to a rockslide at 1.5 miles. Cross it and enter a green meadow 200 yards wide bisected by cascading Perkons Creek, with the lake's headwall looming close ahead. Beyond the meadow climb steeply through thinning timber and increasingly lush understory, fording a rivulet and then into another meadow. Switchback twice to another rivulet at 2.3 miles, then climb steeply in 9 switchbacks, then erratically to a steep slope of white granite boulders strewn in a field of orange paintbrush. Loop right around fallen logs, then left into a cirque and cross it to reach a second, and above it level out on a grassy bench at 3 miles, where the trail fades and the jagged snow-streaked headwall begs to be scratched. Angle 45 degrees left for 200 feet and look down on Perkons Lake 150 yards below. Just stroll down the slope from here.

Best camping is along the outlet creek. The lake's steep, forested shoreline means spinning gear or a float tube for hikers wanting 8 to 11-inch trout for dinner, which feed about 80 feet from shore.

Perkons Lake

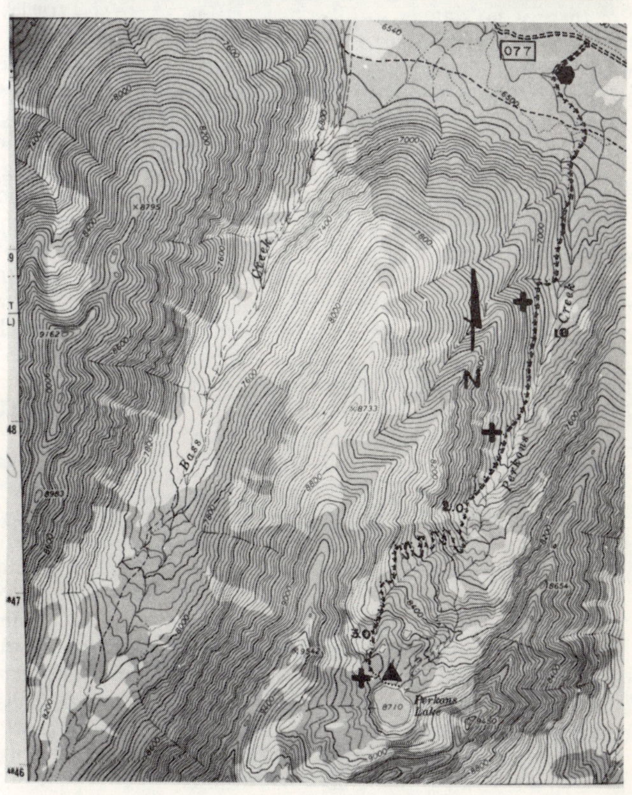

7 BASS LAKES

Distance: 4.9 miles
Elevation gain: 2,340 feet
High point: 8,880 feet
Allow 4 hours
Open July to mid-October
Topographic map:
 U.S.G.S. Marshall Peak
 7.5′ 1964
 U.S.G.S. Newman Peak
 7.5′ 1970
 U.S.G.S. Ross Peak
 7.5′ 1964

Upper Ross Fork Road was built by a rancher named Turner in the late '20's who ran sheep in the area. He procured rainbow trout fry from the game department and in 1936 packed them in milk cans on mules to Ross Fork, Perkons, and Bass Lakes. Forty years later lower Bass Lake still provides excellent angling for rainbow trout to 13 inches, though only intermittent traces remain of the last half of Turner's pack trail. But there is no danger to hikers of getting lost in Bass Creek's narrow valley as they hike through meadows and progressively thinning timber after the trail fades. Because access is more difficult than to Perkons, little evidence of human use was found around the lakes in '76. These tiny patches of blue water sit at the base of cliffs on a grassy bench with flower-spangled meadow forming their shores—a lovely place to camp.

Follow directions to trail No. 6 and continue on the road another mile to a small sign on the left stating Bass Cr. Trail No. 61 Bass Lakes 4 Miles. Park in shade beside the sign. Looking south, the trail begins 10 feet right of the sign, faint but blazed on trees.

Walk south 40 feet, then veer right through a clearing until the trail becomes distinct at its far edge and leads through woods to the Ross Fork's wide gravel bed. Aim for a blazed tree with a clearing showing behind it. Wind across sage and grass into woods with a pineneedle understory with Bass Creek babbling on your left. Climb gently for .5 mile along the creek, then climb erratically to a clearing at .7 mile. Across the creek rocky bluffs rise; on the right firs tuft between rocky promontories. Pass through a shady grove and climb steeply away from the creek to a clearing of shoulder-high willows

and alders at 1 mile. Angular boulders protrude above the brush and pikas tilt back their teddy bear heads and bleat. Climb moderately beside the creek through a slot on the valley's left side, where the lower valley's dry, spacious ambience changes to a lush snugness, as along the green-grassed creek bank crisp spruce and firs replace droopy-boughed Douglas fir. The left slope is neat and lawn-like, the right a jagged canyon wall with trees clinging for dear life. At 1.4 miles pass through a line of trees into a meadow and in .6 mile reach a rockslide where you cross to the left bank and climb into a second grassy amphitheatre. Descend a few yards and cross to the right bank at 2.5 miles; the trail is washed out for 25 yards here, but continue another .3 mile to a fork, ignoring the left going to an old sheepherders camp and veer right 60 feet uphill from a patch of false hellebore on a fading trail. Stay above the trees on the left, and cross a 2-acre patch of hellebore and angle 45 degrees left. Look about 70 yards downhill and see a distinct section of trail. Follow it over a treeless knoll to a blazed tree beside a gully. Wind along a faint trail between stunted blazed conifers over rocky ground for .2 mile, then angle 45 degrees right between 2 large boulders into another huge meadow where elk summer. Climb moderately along the left tree margin where the trail sporadically reappears and at 3.7 miles pass between a cube-shaped boulder on the right and forest on the left. Enter stunted trees, then tall ones, and finally break out into a small marshy meadow. Angle right to drier ground as you traverse the hillside, cross a brook at 4.5 miles and immediately climb up a steep hill; it is dry and littered with logs. The old blazed trail is here, but don't waste effort looking for it. At the hill's top veer left to the creek and follow it to the upper lake, strikingly beautiful turquoise color with a cliff bracing its far shore and the near meadow bright with paintbrush and asters. Strategically-placed spruces create a garden effect.

Reach the lower lake by walking right down the meadow. It is larger, the same blue, with wild rainbow trout cruising the shallows. Don't kill a limit to pack out, for the lake lacks reproduction. There is camping at the upper lake and in the meadow between the two and in the trees.

Upper Bass Lake

Lower Bass Lakes Trail, Ross Fork Valley below

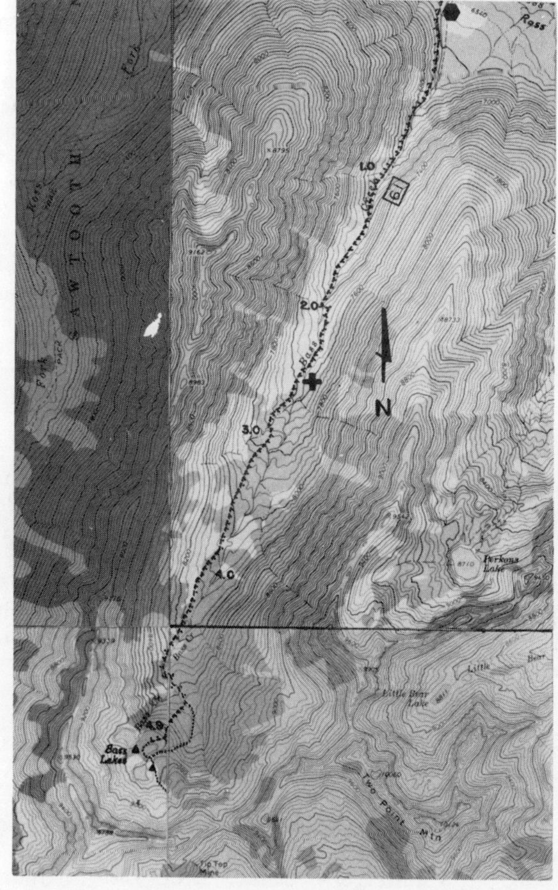

8 ROSS FORK LAKES

Distance: 5.3 miles
Elevation gain: 1,900 feet
High point: 8,600 feet
Allow 3.5 hours
Open July to early October
Topographic maps:
  U.S.G.S. Ross Peak
  7.5′   1964
  U.S.G.S. Atlanta East
  7.5′   1972

Real solitude seldom comes with spectacular alpine scenery stateside these days because of the combined clout of the backpacking and baby booms. But the rugged and remote Ross Fork country receives little traffic because the road to the trailhead is atrocious, and also much of the country is accessible by bush-whacking only. But with wild trout in the lakes and goats, deer, and a few elk roaming the basin, it is a good choice for a 4-day outing. From the ridge above Lake No. 4 there's a stunning view down Willow Creek's gorge, and from any of the scramble-up peaks you can see over numberless ridges west to Boise, north to the Sawtooths, and east to the Pioneers.

Follow directions in hike No. 7 and continue on the jeep trail past the Bass Lakes sign about another .8 mile to a cabin on the left near a large gravel washout. In 100 feet the road forks: bear left across the creek and a 150-yard-wide swath of gravel and up the bank to a sign at the woods' edge stating Ross Fork Trail left. Drive another mile into forest past two cabins on the left to the road's end in a clearing.

Climb gently in a close forested canyon with the creek rushing 20 feet away on the right. At .3 mile veer right away from the creek into dense woods and lush grass understory, and with clear views of steep, rocky, forested slopes on both sides, cross 3 clearings to reach a large meadow tilting from left to right with the creek flowing in its center. Two miles ahead a rounded peak tops 9,000 feet.

Dip across the creek to the left bank and climb steeply 250 yards to a sign stating Ross Fork Lake No. 2 2 miles to the right, Lake No. 4 4 miles left. Bear left climbing moderately with frequent steep pitches through hemlock and fir woods and dry forest floor, with cliffs visible past treetops. Where the trail fractures around fallen timber at 1.7 keep right, watching for old pale Forest Service blazes, then level out across a wide meadow only to reach dense timber again at 3.5 miles beside an avalanche swath of scrub conifers. Climb steeply left, then right and descend winding under tall firs into a clearing and veer 40 yards right on a faint trail, then left through a patch of scrub fir to a sheep camp at 4.0 miles.

Now climb steeply left without switchbacks, watching for blazes for .4 mile, then ease to moderate across a 2-acre meadow, then into timber at the base of a wooded headwall. Cross to Ross Fork's right bank and climb steeply straight uphill on good trail for .1 then switchback raggedly twice in .2 mile to reach a meadow and Ross Fork at 5.1 miles. About 120 yards before the creek the trail subtly forks; look northwest and spot crossing a knoll the trail which quickly becomes distinct and leads to lake No. 4. It's quite shallow, with grassy hills on two sides and cliffs at the far side. Campsites are along the northeast shore. Its limited population of cutthroats to 11'' make feeding forays out of the deep west end into the shallows.

To make a loop trip through all the lakes, follow the trail from No. 4's shore north 1 mile to No. 3, somewhat larger and containing both rainbows and cutthroats to 2½ pounds. From here to lake No. 2 it's cross-country. I suggest camping at No. 2 (a reproducing population of rainbows) and making a day trip to No. 1 and Leggit Lake west across the divide, then following the trail from No. 2 down to the main trail and thence to your car when you decide to leave. There are 3 unnamed lakes over the ridge west of Ross Fork Lakes that may contain trout.

Ross Fork Lake #2

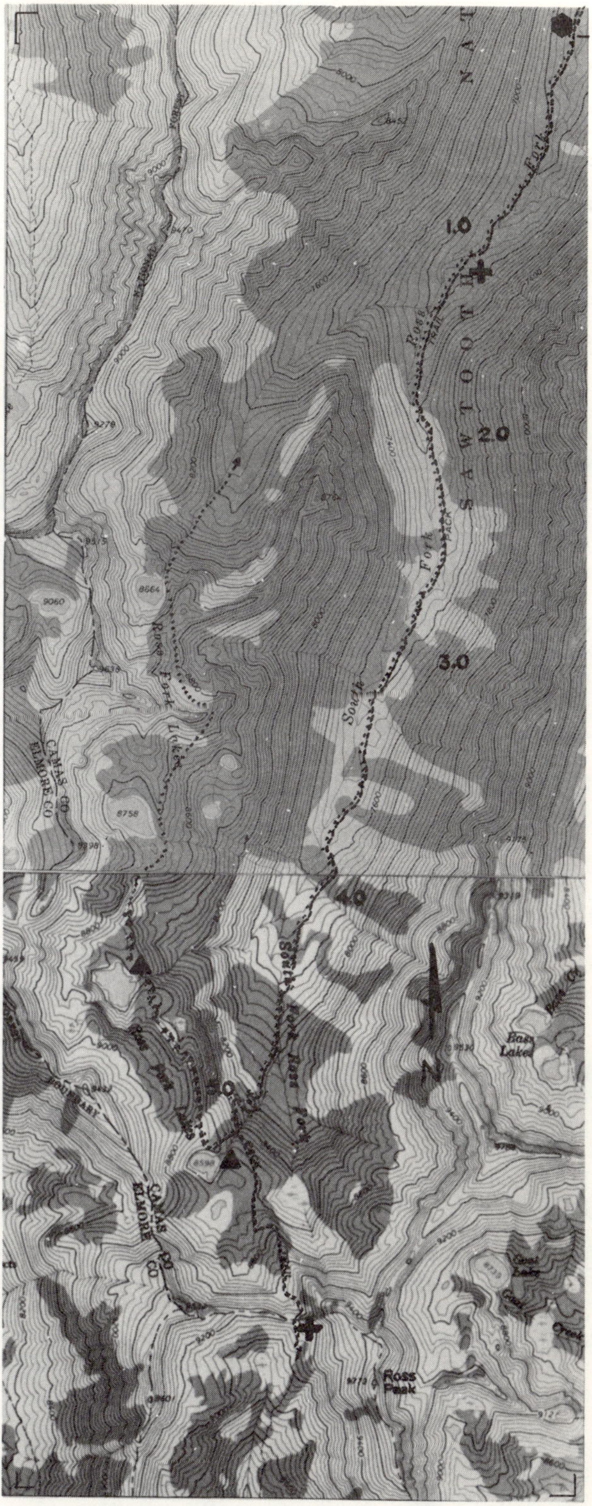

9 KANE LAKE

Distance: 4.3 miles
Elevation gain: 1,650 feet
High point: 9,240 feet
Allow 3 hours
Open July through October
Topographic map:
  U.S.G.S. Phi Kappa Mnt.
  7.5'   1967

Kane Lake, a milky-turquoise gem set in a craggy cirque of white rock, may well be the most beautiful high mountain lake in Idaho, depending on the beholder's aesthetic preferences. Throw in a waterfall splashing into the lake, a stunning giant mountain, a narrow alpine valley shouting with red and purple and yellow wildflowers, and wild cutthroat and rainbow trout, and you have the prototypical Rocky Mountain hiking trail. Though one of the most popular trails near Sun Valley, the Forest Service has had the good sense not to "improve" the trail beyond its delightful primitive state.

From the sign in downtown Ketchum drive approximately 19.5 miles over Trail Creek Road to a sign stating Kane Creek and Canyon and turn right onto a dirt track. In one mile keep left at a fork, drive 1.3 miles to another fork and bear right, then at 2.2 miles bear left at another fork and continue to road's end at a turnaround at 4.9 miles beside Kane Creek.

Cross the creek and walk the old road a half mile to a fork and sign directing you left to the Kane Canyon Trail. On the right rears a craggy, double-faced mountain less than a half mile away. Dead ahead an 11,000-foot headwall with snowfields nestled on sloping talus below its razor spine curves out of sight behind treetops. From the sign walk left 200 yards to where the road cramps left and a sign points straight ahead to Kane Lake. Undulate through dry lodgepole for 0.4 mile and at 1 mile enter a lush meadow affording a perfect picture of the 11,800-foot peak on the right. Walk 0.2 mile through the meadow with Kane creek close on the right, then veer left into woods, twisting and dipping through pine-duff forest floor for 0.8 mile, then climb steeply for another 0.3 mile. Level off briefly and cut right to the creek at 2.3 miles at the very base of the mountain. Climb moderately in heavy shade beside the creek, here a staircase of waterfalls linking limpid pools. Climb erratically another 0.6 mile around rocks and downed timber to a knobby rock, then descend into woods and across a rivulet into a flower-bedecked clearing at the base of a white rockslide at 2.9 miles.

Tilt your head back to scan the spectacular cliffs close on your right. The trail becomes a weaving of several strands for 0.7 mile between the timber's edge and the rockslides on the left. The grassy trailside is resplendent with flowers. At 3.6 miles confront a wall of jumbled granite, with Kane Creek cascading down on your right. Angle left along the left edge of a line of conifers for 0.4 mile to the ridgetop, where trees obscure the lake. Aim for the sharply pointed peak to the right, winding downhill through woods to reach the lake in 300 yards. Campsites abound in the lake basin, but if the mosquitoes are bad look for a site near the lake along the eastern shore.

Though Kane Lake has no natural reproduction, its rainbow and cutthroat trout grow fast and large. Early morning fishing is sometimes better than late afternoon, and midge hatches are frequent. Trees along the north and east shores make a float tube or waders a definite asset to the flyfisherman.

Unnamed peak from Kane Lake Trail

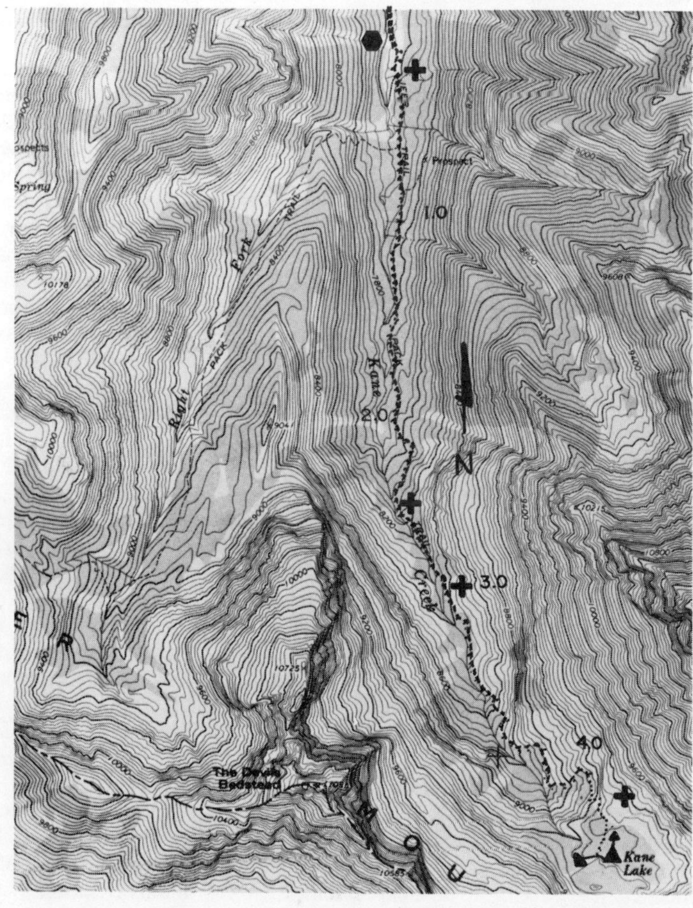

10 SURPRISE VALLEY

Distance: 4.1 miles
Elevation gain: 2,480 feet
High point: 10,160 feet
Allow 4 hours
Open July to mid-October
Topographic map:
    U.S.G.S. Standhope Peak
    7.5′   1967

Surprise Valley is a U-shaped glacial trough tucked 10,000 feet up on the side of Fall Creek Canyon. Watch carefully for blazes once you leave Fall Creek, as the trail receives scant use. Consequently, solitude can be found in these broad meadows bisected by a clear, fishless creek. The riot of wildflowers blooming here in July and early August are almost painfully beautiful to behold. The trail through the upper valley is faint, but you can't get lost. It ends at the upper lake, deeper and colder than the lower one. Standhope peak, a perfect 4-sided arete, rises from it, and this is a good side to scale it without climbing equipment. As one traverses the valley stunning views of Fall Creek Canyon are possible by walking and looking over the right rim. Big Blue Grouse thunder up in exceptional numbers here, and goats graze right down to the valley floor. No trout were present in either lake in '76, and the upper trail is impassable to horses.

Follow directions in trail No. 12 and where the trail forks right to Moose Lake at 1.2 miles keep left. Climb erratically but never steeply through tall forest with a dry floor jackstrewn with logs among boulders. At 1.6 miles the trail fractures around a log jam, then coalesces. Go up a steep pitch, then climb moderately to a sign nailed to a tree on the left at 1.8 miles. Watch carefully for this fork: I give the sign another winter to live. Get a drink from the creek on your right, then go left from the sign, climbing in 7 steep, sometimes faint switchbacks, then climb uphill without them, watching for blazes to help you stay on the faint trail as it turns abruptly left, descends a few feet, then swings steeply right. Make 13 more very steep switchbacks, then wind through conifers ground-collared with dwarf spruce for 30 feet. Now, with a 250-foot cliff on your right and a ragged ridgeline showing through the trees ahead scale a steep hill and at 2.5 miles enter a small meadow. Skirt its right edge to a spring that irrigates the meadow and give yourself an icecream headache by slurping its water. In clear view now is Surprise Valley's eastern wall weathered into spires and protruding vertical spines.

From the spring pick up the trail on the 5-foot knoll sloping left and enter a grove and follow a rivulet's right bank for 40 yards, then cut 90 degrees right up a sage ridge, cross another meadow following blazes, and climb erratically over a dry knoll. Close on the left a rocky slope rises; skirt its base for 300 yards and descend into a swale, then angle left over a rise into another meadow where the trail disappears. Pick it up at the far side and stagger from blaze to blaze along the left slope's base, then angle right weaving through boulders and a few scraggly trees. Keep to the valley's right side here to avoid a rockslide in its center and at 4.1 miles descend into a large meadow holding the shallow, clear lower lake. There are several grassy campsites along its inlet. For a spectacular view of Fall Creek Canyon follow the outlet right.

Head for the upper lake by skirting the lower one's right side and, staying in the meadow between the creek and the cliffs on the right climb steeply several hundred yards, then descend into the upper valley, a 400-yard wide lawn treeless except along the left edge, and spangled with wildflowers. Hike along the valley's right side away from the creek for firmer footing for another mile and reach a grassy hill where the creek angles right into a little canyon. Cross it and angle left uphill and reach the lake, very blue and mirroring Standhope whose toes are rooted in the far shore.

Surprise Valley Lake #1

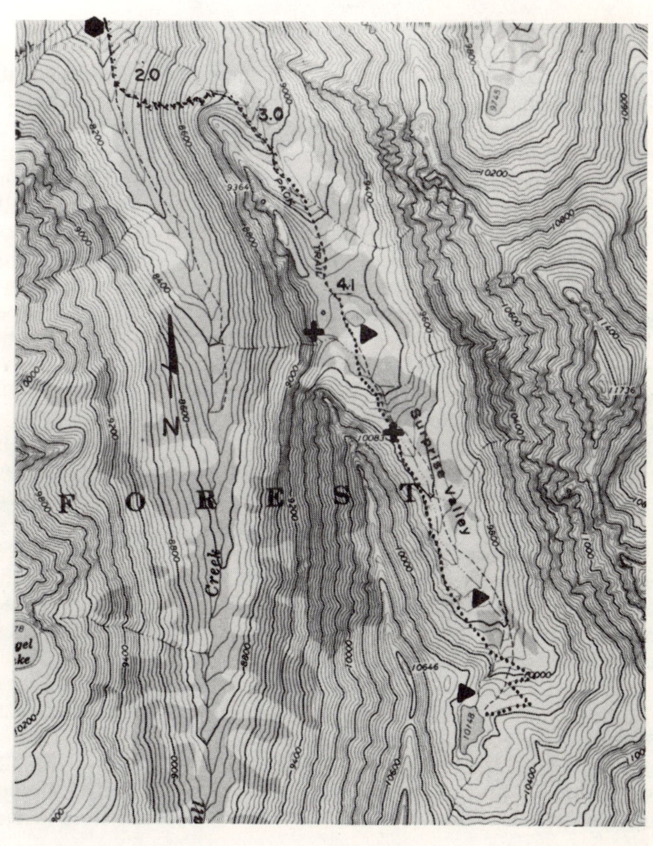

11 FALL CREEK VALLEY

Distance: 5.4 miles
Elevation gain: 1,715 feet
High point: 9,400 feet
Allow 3 hours
Open late June to mid-October
Topographic map:
  U.S.G.S. Standhope Peak
  7.5′   1967

God bless blowdowns. It is because of them that the remote, altogether lovely alpine valley at Fall Creek's head seldom sees hikers. Hope the Forest Service never clears the trees blocking this long, narrow glacial trough with steep walls timbered on their lower slopes but rising above timberline into snowy rock summits. At its head a high headwall with two permanent snowfields gives one a sense of looming omnipotence. Three lakes lie in the rocks of the right valley wall and can be reached by scrambling along a waterfall tumbling into Fall Creek. Since the poor trail and absence of trout in the creek screen out most hikers and fishermen, this is an ideal spot to get shed of fellow alpinists and learn the difference between the sound the wind makes in the trees as compared to grass. Meditators' Mecca, in other words. Because of the blowdowns don't attempt to hike out late or after dark, as even a flashlight won't keep you from leaving an eye impaled on a spruce limb.

Follow directions in trail No. 12 to the trailhead and No. 10 to the left fork to Surprise Valley, but keep right instead on the main trail. Parallel Fall Creek's succession of pools through lodgepole and boulder-strewn understory, with cliffs show-ing close through the trees on both sides. At 1.8 miles angle left steeply for 150 yards then ease to gentle for .4 mile to where the trail fractures around blowdowns. Cross a brook tumbling down from Surprise Valley and climb erratically in woods until at 2.6 miles you angle right to the creek from where the distant headwall and snowfields are visible. Soon the valley widens in a blush of lushness split by the creek, with Standhope Peak on the left and another huge rock mountain on the right. Weave through a thin line of firs arcing across the valley to another clearing at 3.0 miles. From here on the trail exists in fragments, so be sure and hit it in good light.

Angle gently left from the clearing and in 200 yards enter timber where the trail forks. Follow blazes right for .1 mile to a rockslide and leave the creek and climb through woods to a willow-choked bog. Angle 45 degrees left for 35 feet, then right through an opening and faint wet trail through willows to a patch of timber, across another park to a blaze on its far side. Weave through 400 yards of trees, then cut left and walk the edge between trees and rock to another park, a grove of firs, and into the basin at approximately 5.4 miles at the foot of a wall so close and steep it startles you.

Fall Creek Valley

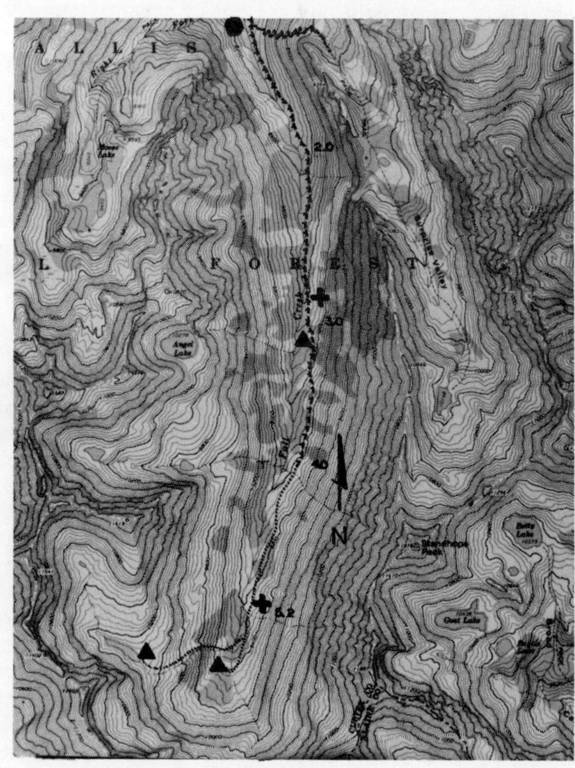

12 MOOSE LAKE

Distance: 3.4 miles
Elevation gain: 1,660 feet
High point: 9,345 feet
Allow 2.5 hours
Open late June to mid-October
Topographic map:
U.S.G.S. Standhope Peak
7.5′ 1967

Like most trails in the Pioneers, this one starts in sage and grass, winds along a creek, the foliage getting greener and thicker as you climb. It's divided neatly into thirds: along Fall Creek in open timber, switchbacking through shady woods along Moose Creek, and climbing through meadows with high glaciated cliffs ahead. Tree-lined Moose Lake is large, with an upper lake and spectacular snow-streaked headwall. Its excellent reproducing population of rainbow and brook trout average 9 inches and can be caught by novice anglers. Forest and several small meadows mean several parties can camp here out of sight and earshot of each other.

Drive either 25 miles from Sun Valley or 44 miles from Mackay on the Sun Valley-Mackay road No. 51 and turn onto the Copper Basin Road at the sign and drive 2 miles to another sign and turn right heading for Wildhorse Guard Station. In 3.2 miles turn left at the Fall Creek sign and after slightly over .2 mile turn left across Fall Creek if you have 4-wheel drive or a VW bug, etc., and drive 2 miles on a rough narrow track to a turnaround beside Left Fork Fall Creek, where a sign marks the Fall Creek Trail.

If you're driving a passenger car don't cross Fall Creek but right after turning off the Wildhorse Road continue straight ahead for 600 yards and park in a grove of aspens. From here a shady trail along Fall Creek will take you to the Left Fork Fall Creek, where you'll cross to Fall Creek's left bank and reach the parking area and sign mentioned above.

From the parking area cross the left fork Fall Creek and immediately reach a fork and keep right descending across a sage flat to the creek in 160 yards. You are heading up a narrow forested valley with a steep spired peak on the right that diminishes into the distance in a rocky spine. Veer left from the creek across a small meadow shagged with willow clumps and small pines. At .3 miles climb erratically through open woods and dry forest floor to finally dip to a fork at 1.2 miles admist scattered boulders. A sign, Moose Lake right, may or may not be leaning against a tree. Go right across Fall Creek and pause for a drink, then make 3 long steep switchbacks across a brushy avalanche path, traverse steeply left for .6 mile, then abruptly veer right. Stop and look through the screen of trees at the rugged eastern wall of Fall Creek's canyon, forested on its lower half, the upper gouged into spires and thin horizontal spines. That break in the crest is the entrance to Surprise Valley.

Climb moderately through woods with a forest floor of dead gray logs, rocks, and dwarf spruce, with the creek within earshot on your left as you enter N. F. Fall Creek's canyon at 2.2 miles. Left across the creek a huge rock knob several hundred feet high rears from meadow, a common geological structure in the Pioneers. Traverse a talus slope dotted with trees and descend to the creek rushing through its verdant sleeve of brush and flowers at 2.4 miles. Cross it and a band of dense woods and a bog and enter a broad valley with a pyramidal peak on the left and a rounded granite hill bristly with firs ahead. Wind steeply up it between smooth convex granite humps, ignoring a fork cutting right towards the creek's murmur and keeping left to the ridgetop at 2.8 miles. Descend into thick woods, then quickly into a breathtaking, meadowed amphitheatre. Towering rock escarpments encircle the valley a scant mile ahead. Skirt the meadow's left edge where a meandering creek harbors trout as arrow-swift and skittish as thoroughbreds and climb steeply for 150 yards through woods to reach the lake at 3.4 miles.

Besides the meadow you just passed there is camping along the lake's south and west shores, and around the upper lake accessible by walking along Moose's left shore. The trout in Moose feed all day extensively on midge pupae and adults in the shallows at the north end. Waders are a must for flyfishermen. All brook trout, which naturally reproduce, should be kept to keep this burgeoning population balanced.

Angler at Moose Lake outlet

Moose Lake

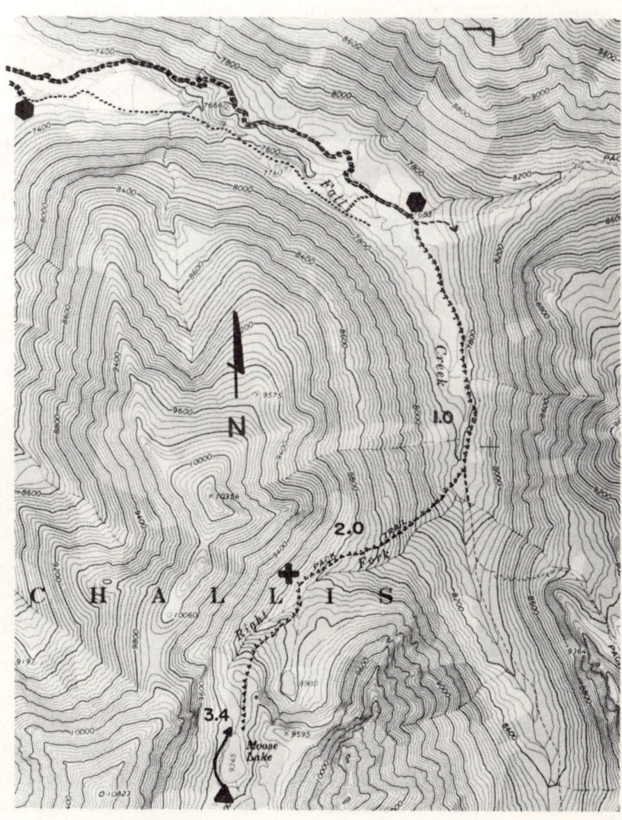

13 BOULDER LAKE

Distance: 4 miles
Elevation gain: 2,250 feet
High point: 9,570 feet
Allow 3.5 hours
Open late June through October
Topographic map:
  U.S.G.S. Standhope Peak
  7.5′ 1967
  U.S.G.S. Phi Kappa Mnt.
  7.5′ 1967

Boulder Lake is the prototypical Pioneer Mountains hike, beginning in firs and sage where one can see the entire mountain at the start: the forested lower slopes giving way 4,000 feet above to glaciated rock peaks, all looking a bit dry. And then suddenly, in the upper half of the hike, one enters a fairy kingdom hidden from below, of a shallow lush valley near the top of the rock peak that even up here is still a headwall 2,000 feet high, and water everywhere in creeks and alpine lakes. Boulder Lake's outlet waters a meadow with such a stream flowing through it, and the walls of its box canyon are sheer, pale, granite-sedimentary conglomerate that become more impressive the closer one comes to the lake. Washington Lake lies even higher and to the right of Boulder and can be reached by a short hike. This is a good afternoon hike because the trail is shaded most of the way, and its 13″ rainbows feed mostly in the evening.

Drive 25 miles from Sun Valley on Trail Creek Road and turn right at the Copper Basin Wildhorse Creek sign and in 2 miles turn right at another fork and sign stating Wildhorse Creek. In another 3.8 miles spot a sign on the right partially screened by brush that says Boulder Lake and turn right into a campground and park under trees.

You'll need tennis shoes to ford Wildhorse Creek at the gravel bar between you and the distant mouth of Boulder Creek's canyon due west. Clamber up the far bank and angle right for about 20 yards and intersect the trail where it crosses a sage flat—there may be a sign. Follow it into woods with a dry pine-needle understory and climb moderately .3 mile and make 5 steep switchbacks. Traverse moderately with Boulder Creek in a canyon on your left until at .9 mile the canyon opens into a grassy valley dotted with conifers. Climb moderately with the creek occasionally visible, crossing it at 1.5 miles and winding in and out of woods and around granite outcroppings for .4 mile, then angling very steeply away from the creek around a granite knob and through rock-strewn forest to Boulder Creek necklacing down in a series of pools. On the left an arrowhead-shaped peak intervenes between you and the distant headwall that encircles the valley with a ragged glacier horizontally streaking its center. Close on the right a high flat-topped scarp soars 2,100 feet and is grassy even on its highest reaches.

Make several short, steep switchbacks at 2.6 miles and meet the creek and cross to the right bank, ignoring a fork left. Climb gently for 350 yards to a meadow, meander along its right edge for .7 mile, then pass through a line of timber at 3.8 miles, where the trail ends. Boulder Creek is left, cascading down a rocky defile. Cross to its left bank and pick your way over talus for .2 mile and reach the lake.

Best camping is by the outlet and 200 yards right of it. In stormy weather the meadow below the lake would be a more prudent choice. The lake has no natural reproduction, so limit your catch.

Trout leaping, Boulder Lake

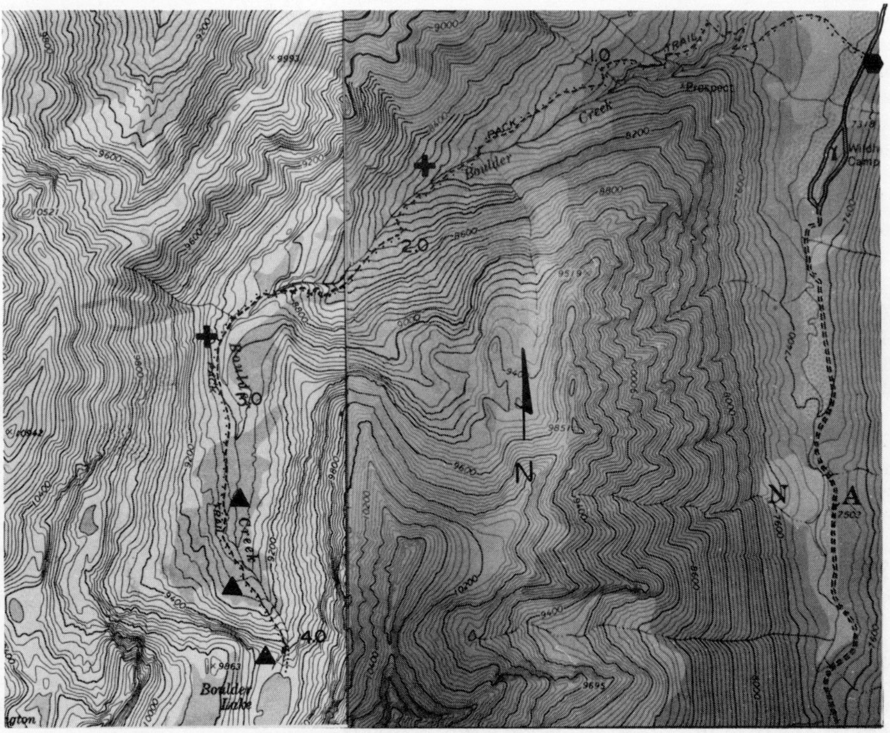

14 BOX CANYON

Distance: 3.7 miles
Elevation gain: 2,400 feet
High Point: 10,000 feet
Allow 3 hours
Open July to October
Topographic map:
U.S.G.S. Gray's Peak
7.5′ 1967

This hike with a stunning view of the Pioneer and Lost River Ranges, and the rugged headwater canyons of the Little Wood River, traces the Wood River's east fork to its source in a spacious mountain valley, climbs over a 10,000-foot pass, and drops into Box Canyon, a basin of tilted meadows and lakes sequestered in nooks of its jagged rim. Brook and cutthroat trout swim in Upper Box Canyon Lake, and cutthroats in Windy, Nip 'n Tuck, and Lower Box Canyon. A herd of mule deer summers in the canyon, and goats roam the crags. A rugged loop trip traversing several plant zones can be made by continuing on trail No. 175 down Box Canyon to the Little Wood River, thence down No. 173 beside the river to Iron Mine Creek, and up No. 174 over a 10,000-foot ridge to the Mascot Mine, an eighth-mile from where you parked your car. The distance would be about 15 miles.

From Ketchum drive 5.5 miles south on U.S. 93, or from Hailey drive 6 miles north on U.S. 93, to the sign at the East Fork Wood River Road and drive east for about 7.2 miles to a road fork, road 203 going left

up Hyndman Creek, and No. 118 and you heading right. Drive another 7.7 miles to a gate and cattle guard marking the Mascot Mine property and continue almost another mile to a shallow, grassy slope on the left and park your car; the road goes further, but it's very rough.

Walk along the road that narrows in 0.6 mile to trail by a registration box. Swing left, climbing steeply around a rock bluff and descend into a U-shaped open valley with scattered trees and an arc of woods curving across the valley a mile ahead. Jagged 3,000-foot ridges on both sides converge in an 11,000-foot headwall in the distance. For 0.3 mile climb gently through grass and fields of bluebells, wild parsnip, penstemon, and paintbrush, past a waterfall plunging down from a hanging valley on your left. At 0.8 mile cross a rockslide and enter a crescent of woods where the East Fork is now a brook on the right and pikas scurry for cover, bleating indignantly from a rockslide. At 1.4 miles leave the woods and cross the East Fork amidst a moisture-seeking blush of bluebells and columbines that draw hummingbirds in August. Ahead left is a symmetrical spire resembling the Matterhorn, and issuing from the cliffs around it are 3 waterfalls. After climbing steeply another 0.5 mile reach a sign almost promising Johnstone Pass is only a mile away—straight uphill.

Angle right a short distance from the sign and climb steeply for 0.9 mile in 29 switchbacks in the scattered shade of pines. Clumps of pink and white phlox and pussytoes and alpine forget-me-nots are everywhere. Johnstone Pass is just a 15-foot-wide notch in crumbling rock, and one has the sense of peeping into Box Canyon. Descend for 0.5 mile in 11 very steep switchbacks to the level where the trail forks. You can go left across the creek and uphill to the upper lake (which is visible from the pass), or take the right fork for 0.7 mile, then turn right off the trail, cross the creek, climb through open timber towards that dominant peak with the pyramid-shaped tip, to reach the lower lake.

The trout in the lower lake winterkilled in '75, and the lake hasn't been restocked in '77. The upper lake offers good fishing along its south shore, and the others, reached by contouring from it, offer excellent cutthroat fishing.

Upper Box Canyon Lake

Box Canyon from Johnstone Pass

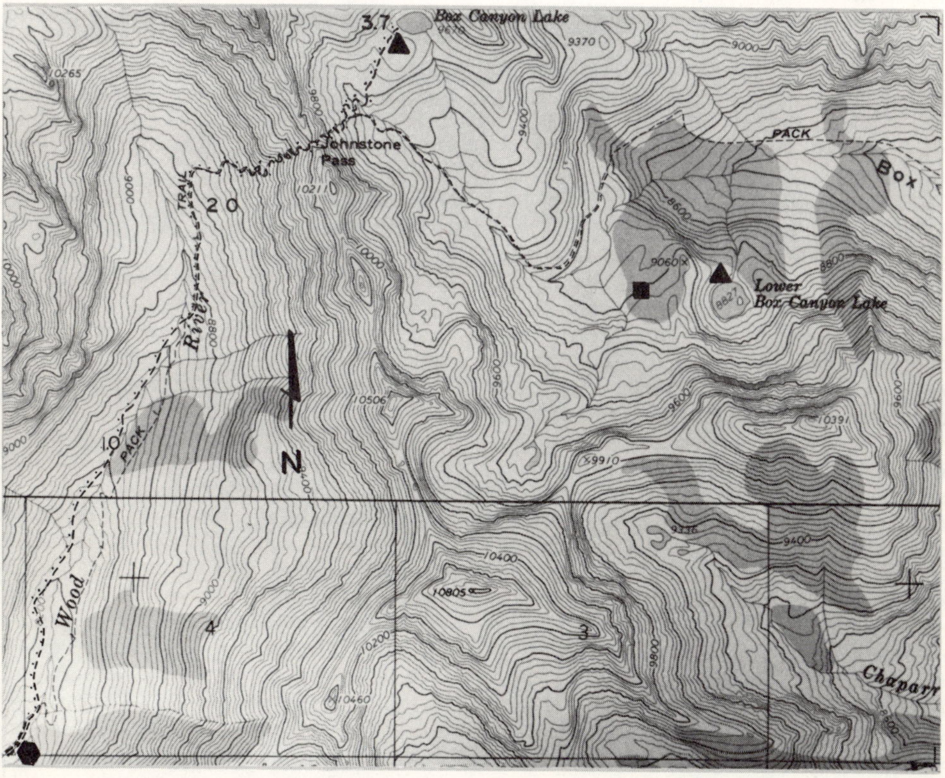

15 BELLAS CANYON TRAIL

Distance: 3.1 miles
Elevation gain: 1,700 feet
High point: 9,400 feet
Allow 2 hours
Open July through October
Topographic map:
  U.S.G.S. Copper Basin
  15′ 1960

The eastern face of the Pioneer Range's rampart in Copper Basin represents a classic study in glaciation, with lateral moraines shouldering each major creek, channeling them down to join together and flow at a right angle to their individual canyons after colliding with the terminal moraine's wall. The highest slopes are riddled with aretes, headwalls, and cirques and hanging valleys. The trail to Bellas Lakes climbs in the bottom of a vanished glacier's trough and leads one to 4 lakes set in depressions interspersed with meadows. White granite and limestone crags and cliffs loom close on all sides. Unfortunately the Forest Service allows grazing even around these lakes at 10,000 feet, and in '76 18 herefords were grazing in the lower lake's inlet, muddying its flow and defecating in it. All the flat ground was grazed and plastered with manure, ruining from July to September most of the campsites and all flowing water supplies. The same situation exists at Betty and Big Lakes, and other letters duplicating mine to the Challis National Forest Headquarters in Challis might help rectify the situation. Above the herefords, goats can be seen, and mule deer bucks bed in the rocks above North Fork Lake to escape insects— insects that feed cutthroat trout in the lakes. The basin's sparse timber facilitates cross-country hiking, and one could spend a leisurely day exploring the several minor basins and meadows.

Drive 25 miles from Sun Valley or 44 from Mackay on the Sun Valley-Mackay Road No. 51 and turn south at the Copper Basin sign and drive 2 miles to a fork and sign stating Copper Basin left. In another 13 miles reach the Copper Basin Loop Road and turn right, drive 4.7 miles to the Bellas Canyon sign and turn right again and in .4 mile park under trees at the road's end.

Intersect the trail on the creek's right bank, then abruptly angle right, climbing moderately through lodgepole and aspen, around boulders and fallen timber with the creek invisible but audible on the left. At .5 mile cross a small sage clearing and ease to a gentle grade on a bench above the creek, walking in grassy woods flecked with flowers and a heavily-wooded hillside across the creek from you. Skirt a meadow's left edge and descend across to Bellas Creek's left bank at .9 miles. Enter dense woods and exit in 120 yards into a park where coyotes are frequently seen hunting mice and gophers. On the left is a dark wall of conifers and right, above the creek's willows, a lateral moraine, foliaged in silver sage with dark lines of pines in gulleys running down its shoulders. Peeping over its rounded crest is a distant angular peak.

At 1.1 miles enter woods again and climb steeply for 350 yards to another meadow, then timber again with an understory of scrub conifers, then another steep meadow. Climb erratically into woods to a fork at 1.8 miles. Go right for .4 mile paralleling the creek and enter a park below a box canyon wall with a black knob at its center. Walk to the creek, get a drink and rest, and climb steeply up its far bank for .2 mile, then traverse left moderately with 2 steep pitches through open whitebark pine woods to a large grassy amphitheatre at 2.7 miles. The cream-colored crest of an awesome ridge looms about two miles ahead, visible over the treetops. Cross the meadow on the level and with the creek cascading down on your left climb moderately to the lower lake at 3.1 miles. It is deep green and partially rimmed by pines, and shelters cutthroat and a few golden trout.

By hiking up the first creek you cross flowing into the lake's right side you'll reach another lake. If you walk almost due north from this shallow tarn for .4 mile through open meadow and forest you'll reach North Fork Lake, whose open shoreline augments flycasting for its native cutthroats to 11 inches. These trout reproduce meagerly in the outlet creek, and should be released to assist the naturally reproducing population—a rarity in alpine lakes.

Copper Basin from Bellas Lakes Trail

Bellas Lake #1

16 BETTY LAKE

Distance: 4.8 miles
Elevation gain: 2,620 feet
High point: 10,379 feet
Allow 5 hours
Open July to October
Topographic maps:
   U.S.G.S. Copper Basin
   15'   1960
   U.S.G.S. Standhope Peak
   7.5'   1967

Hiking to Betty Lake through Broad Canyon is thrilling in several ways. The lower canyon is green with flowers everywhere, with a sweet, pungent balance of meadow and forest scents. But always above this friendly plant texture one sees the harsh, jagged cliffs and peaks of red and bone-white rock holding forth the promise of higher, wilder country to come. The last third of the trail scales a steep face to what seems the roof of the world, treeless tundra with blue lakes sparkling in green lawn. And then by walking to the summit of Standhope Peak above Betty Lake, the view of all the southern Idaho Rockies will fill you with awe. And for lunch, catch your own: cutthroat trout and rainbows from Betty Lake, and cutthroats from Baptie and Goat Lakes. With a 400 mm lens and some judicious stalking you can snap shots of mountain goats that are part of a herd carefully managed by the Idaho Fish and Game Dept.

From a sign in downtown Ketchum drive 25 miles on Trail Creek Road to the Copper Basin road sign and turn south. Or, from Mackay drive 15 miles north on U.S. Alt. 93 and turn left at the Trail Creek Road sign to Sun Valley and drive 29 miles and turn south on the Copper Basin Road. Continue 13 miles and turn right at the sign stating Starhope Canyon and Creek. Drive 8 miles and turn right again at the Broad Canyon Trail sign, crawl on a dirt track 0.5 mile and turn left at a fork, and go 0.3 mile to a spring flowing from a pipe on the left berm. Park here, for there is no room ahead.

The road narrows after a few hundred feet, and you walk an undulating, twisting trail through spruce, fir, and lodgepole woods, catching glimpses of the creek on the right flowing through grass and willows, and beyond it the opposite ridge, a rounded lateral moraine littered with stones and nubbled with silver sage, with lines of conifers in gullies intersecting at angles. After 0.7 mile the trail forks at the creek; take the left one, crossing the shallows to the north bank. Immediately cross a large meadow yellow with arrowleaf balsamroot and in the next 0.8 mile cross a series of small meadows, then meet the creek again. Climb moderately away from the creek through dense lodgepoles, ignoring a sign at 1.8 miles pointing left to Bear Creek, and bear right up a ridge above the creek, with views of reddish peaks on the left, until at 2.8 miles you break out into a magnificent open valley with jagged white peaks above forest in the background. Cross to the creek's left bank and traverse erratically across seeping springs steeped in hellebore, penstemon, and cinquefoil, and angle steeply uphill into a tilted meadow with cliffs shouldering on the left and a pyramid-shaped peak ahead. Enter scrub timber rampant with flowers, leap the creek at 3.8 miles, and climb in steep switchbacks to a meadow hazed with blue lupine. Climb steeply for 0.5 mile into 2 more basins, reach a fork and bear left following the creek up a steep draw to another basin at 4.5 miles. Skirt its right edge and climb steeply to a hilly slope. The trail disintegrates here, but the highest peak ahead is Standhope, and by climbing toward it arrive at Betty Lake.

Goat and Baptie Lakes can be reached through the draw at the lake's S.E. edge. Both support excellent but non-reproducing populations of cutthroat trout that grow fat on zooplankton. Open shorelines at all the lakes make waders superfluous. There are good campsites at all the lakes, but Betty is exposed to winds, and camping back down the trail in timber would be prudent.

Angler casting for trout at Goat Lake

Goat Lake, above Betty Lake

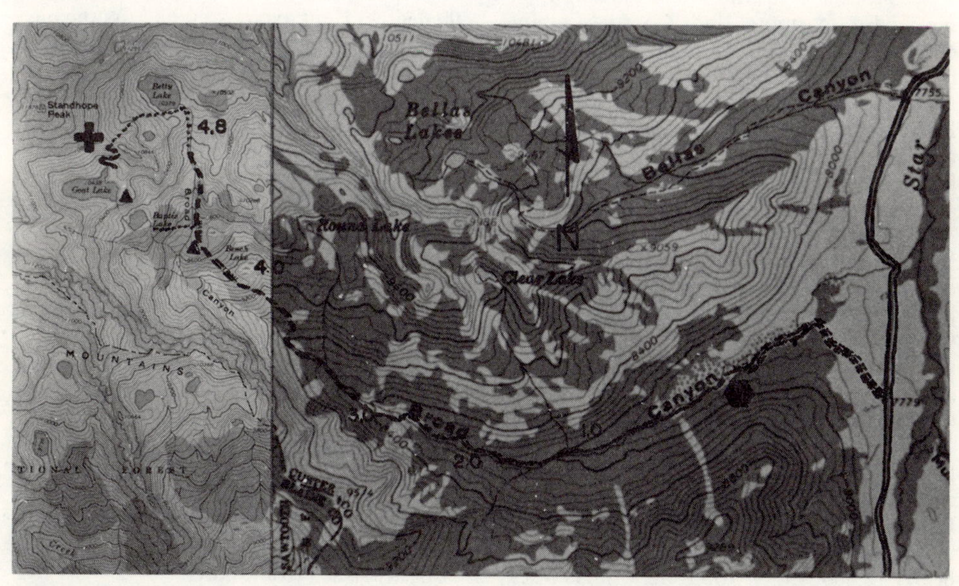

17 BIG LAKE

Distance: 5 miles
Elevation gain: 1,456 feet
High point: 9,480 feet
Allow 3.5 hours
Open July to late October
Topographic map:
  U.S.G.S. Copper Basin
  15′   1960
  U.S.G.S. Muldoon Canyon
  15′   1960

This trail is a sleeper, an unlikely charmer that lures one to her bosom with seductive revelations that eventually elicit exclamations like, "My goodness, I never dreamed you could be like this!" It begins inauspiciously in a rocky, sage-covered high-desert canyon with scattered pines on the walls, but then abruptly enters an amphitheatre carpeted with grass and flowers wicking their verdure from a blue trout stream that the beavers have dammed. Then a steep ascent in lush forest past a colony of big hoary marmots leads to high alpine country and 5 lakes. An excellent 2-day 11-mile loop trip can be made by continuing from Big Lake on a gentle trail to Rough, Round, and Long Lakes, then back to the amphitheatre. Incidentally, Round Lake hosts rare Montana Grayling.

Drive to Copper Basin as in trail No. 16 but continue past the Broad Canyon sign to Star Hope Campground where you'll turn left and climb a hill and descend to Lake Creek in about 3.3 miles. Turn right at the sign and cross a cattle guard and gate and drive along the road another .2 mile to its end and a sign banning autos.

Hike along the road across sage with scattered pines for 1.5 miles to thick woods. Stop and look back for a magnificent view of the Pioneer rampart rising from sage and grass at 7,000 feet to small glaciers and rock at nearly 12,000. Enter woods on a single track now and cross a meadow and rivulet, loop downhill right, then left, and cross a creek as you skirt a willow-choked meadow at 2.2 miles. Beaver ponds in the meadow have brook trout. High rocky peaks loom close above the forest on the right. Meander through woods for .7 mile to a grove of firs and veer left over bare forest floor, watching for blazes, and reach a cabin on the right at 3.1 miles. Enter a wide, high-walled valley dotted with beaver ponds and skirt its left edge to a fence at 3.7 miles and cross it. Turn 90 degrees right and descend across the meadow and cross Lake Creek on logs, negotiate a few feet of bog and willows, then veer left across a rockslide and after 2 switchbacks begin a moderate traverse to the left with sporadic switchbacks that end in a grassy swale with marmots whistling from the rocks on the right. Climb steeply up the swale for 600 yards, level out briefly, then veer right descending through whitebark pines and suddenly reach the lake at 5.0 miles. It is pale blue with unique angular red rocks paving its bottom. Rolling meadow stretches away on all sides, bumping into a line of peaks a half-mile to the west. Shaded campsites are everywhere. If you don't like what you see stroll north over the hill to Golden Lake and fish for rainbow trout. Big Lake has rainbows and cutthroats, Long has rainbows, Rough has both cutts and 'bows, and Round sports them along with grayling. All these lakes can be easily fished from shore.

Hiker, Big Lake Trail

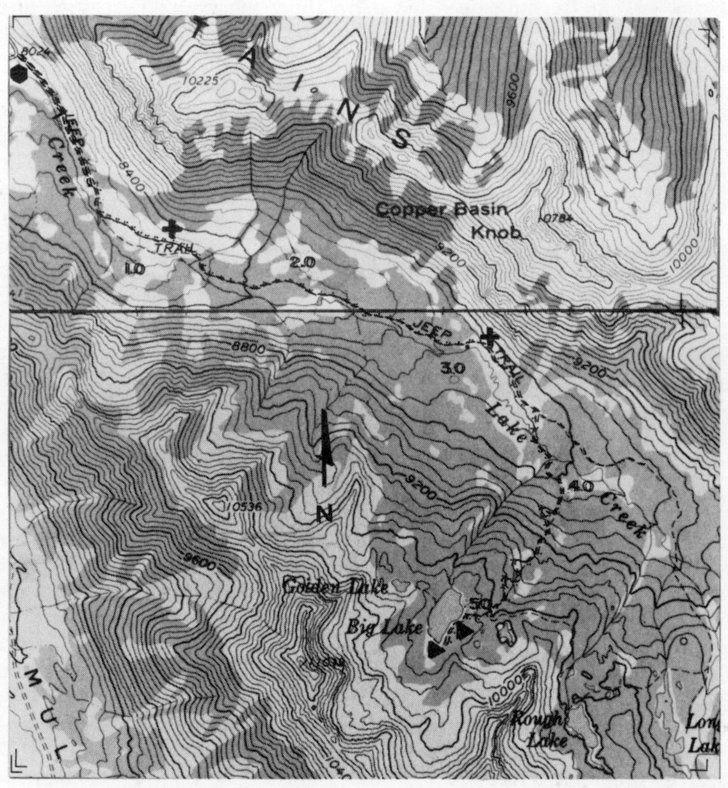

18 AMBER LAKES

Distance: 3.9 miles
Elevation gain: 2,140 feet
High point: 9,100 feet
Allow 4.5 hours
Open late June through October
Topographic map:
  U.S.G.S. Amber Lakes
  7.5′ 1967

At the height of the summer tourist season when popular trails around Sun Valley become somewhat crowded, the hiker experienced in cross-country travel or the novice wishing to try his hand at it without danger of getting lost can find solitude by trekking to Amber Lakes Basin. There is a trail halfway, and then you'll make your own in a narrow, well-defined box canyon. The lower basin is home for mule deer and many blue grouse, and Rocky Mountain Goats clamber along the horseshoe ridge encompassing the valley. From this ridge several possible cross-country routes ray out down to U.S. 93 and the North Fork Road, but these should be attempted only by the experienced. One can also make an alternate trip up the West Fork Trail past the Amber Lakes cutoff for 3.5 miles into the beautiful valley at the creek's head, where a brace of alpine lakes nestle near the headwall's crest.

Drive 7.8 miles north of Sun Valley on U.S. 93 and at a sign marking the North Fork Wood River road turn right and drive 4.0 miles to a fork and keep left to the road's end at 5.2 miles. On the right is a registration box and sign for the North Fork Trail, but you walk left (west), fording the creek and climbing the bank to a sign forbidding cycles, where the trail begins.

Meander for the first 0.2 mile through dense woods with a grassy floor speckled with monkshood, sego lilies, and paintbrush. Abruptly begin climbing moderately past a meadow on your left, level off opposite a jackstraw tangle of logs at .6 mile, and continue climbing moderately another .6 miles in a narrow forested canyon with sheer scarps visible 2,000 feet above on your right.

At 1.3 miles reach an avalanche path of short, twisted trees and see on your left Amber Creek tumbling down. Walk ahead a short distance to a clearing and fork, the right going away from the creek. Take the left, just a trace, into the clearing, aiming for 2 small cairns on the far side. Cross 2 small water courses, then the main creek, and another course, which you follow downstream about 60 yards to blazes on a tree. Veer right here onto an unmistakable right-of-way cut through lodgepoles, veer left for 150 yards to Amber Creek, cross it and turn right to climb a very steep, narrow trail through thick timber and emerge at a rockslide at 1.6 miles.

You're looking slightly downhill into a brushy basin half a mile long. The ridge at its head blocks your view of the high country that cradles Amber Lakes. Hug the base of the rockslide on your left and climb 400 yards on the trail to where it fractures and fades. Horses and people have made several inconstant paths, but the general route is high on this ridge above the creek and its brush. Traverse for .7 mile until you see a small grassy basin on your right, drop into it and cross to Amber Creek's west bank. Follow the creek 200 yards over a low ridge into another basin, then another and then 2 more. The creek curves right out of the last basin to the upper lake, the prettier of the two. The meadow back down the creek offers several camping sites. To reach the lower lake on your return, climb through the trees at the upper lake's west end and veer right through a rocky draw to the lake, and then follow its outlet down to Amber Creek. There are presently no trout in either lake.

Looking south over Boulder Mountains from Amber Lakes

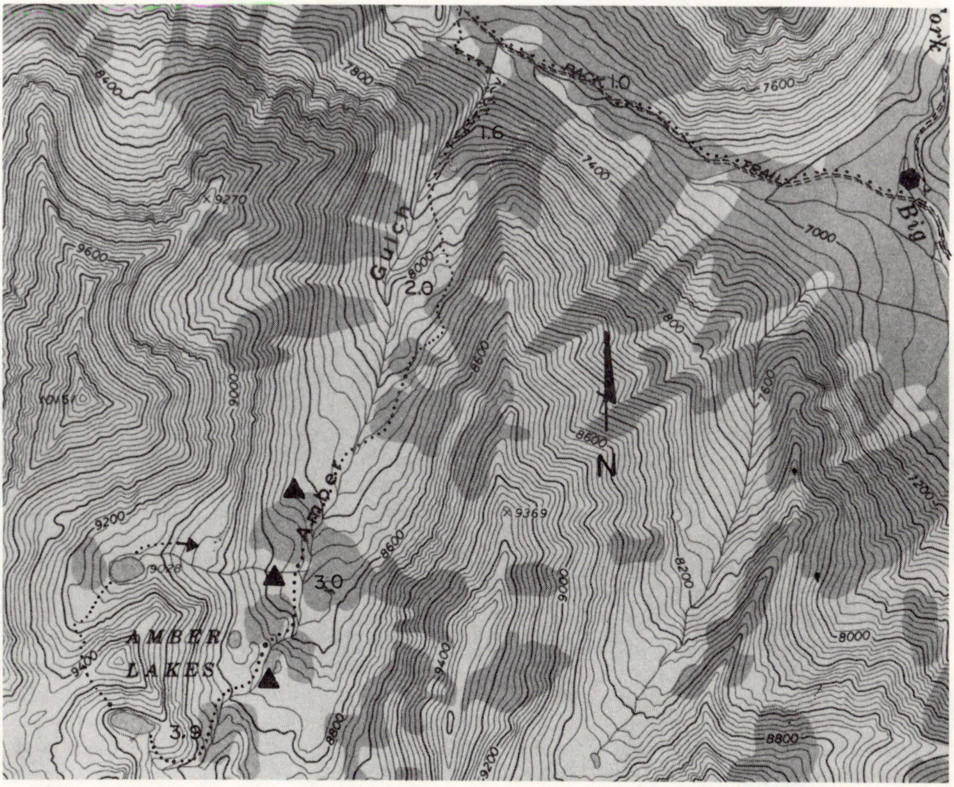

19 NORTON LAKES

Distance: 2.6 miles
Elevation gain: 1,250 feet
High point: 8,950 feet
Allow 1.5 hours
Open late June through October
Topographic map:
U.S.G.S. Baker Peak
7.5′ 1970

This hike is ideal for an afternoon outing because it is shaded and short, although steep. Both Norton Lakes hold excellent populations of rainbow trout, and 4 goats and several grouse were seen in '77 at the upper lake. Wildflowers are especially abundant here in July, and the peaks above the verdant slopes are the most rugged in the Smoky Mountains. By climbing the lower lake's western shore along a swale, then veering west, you can reach Big Lost Lake, and below it Smoky Lake, and finally follow Smoky's outlet creek down to the Norton Creek trail and back to your car. By scrambling up the north slope of the upper lake you can see Miner Lake, and drop down to it if you wish.

From Sun Valley drive about 15 miles north to the Baker Creek Road No. 162 sign and turn left. Drive 6 miles and turn right at a sign stating Norton Lakes 4, Prairie Lakes 6. Drive another mile and park in a gravel turnaround. The trail begins at the Norton Lakes sign.

Hike along the canyon's left side, the right slope rising to a ridgetop of eroded rock parapets. The grade is moderate with steep pitches, winding through lodgepole woods with a grass-and-wildflower understory to a bench 70 feet above Norton Creek at 0.3 mile. A short distance ahead dip across a tributary, then angle left away from the creek into tall woods for 0.7 mile, make 2 switchbacks, then climb another 0.6 mile through dry sage and grass to a rockslide. The creek is a faint rushing sound on the right, and the jagged righthand ridge is now a scant 400 yards away. Angle steeply left into a small basin, level out for 60 yards, then traverse to the lip of another verdant basin and descend to the creek at 2.3 miles and cross it. Turn left and climb steeply another 0.3 mile to reach the lower lake at 2.6 miles. To reach the upper lake, continue right along the shore to the inlet, parallel it 80 feet, switchback right, then left and cross to the west bank and enter the upper lake's cirque.

There is more camping room around the upper lake than the lower, but it is windier up there. The trout in both lakes frequent the south, west, and east shores. They are small, but can be elusive because they feed on midge pupae most of the summer and size 18-24 flies and 6X leaders are required to entice them.

Meadow on Lower Norton Lakes Trail

Breakfast at Norton Lakes

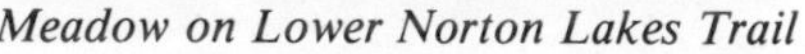

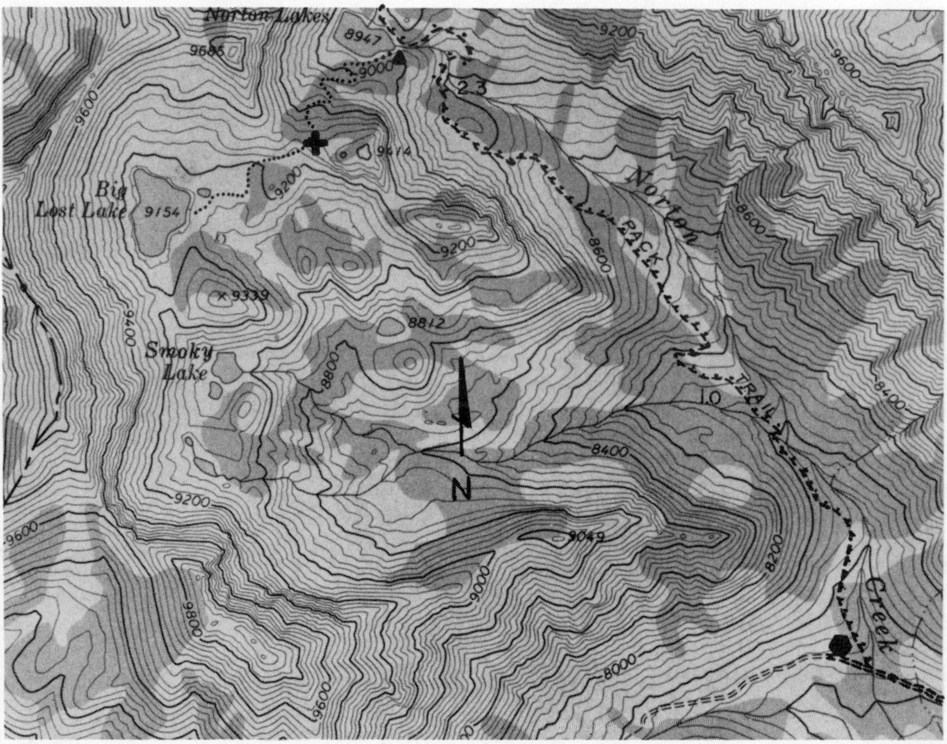

20 MINER LAKE

Distance: 3.7 miles
Elevation gain: 1,170 feet
High point: 8,770 feet
Allow 2.5 hours
Open mid-June to November
Topographic map:
U.S.G.S. Galena
7.5'   1970

In spite of its proximity to Sun Valley, the Miner Lake Trail is narrow and relatively uncrowded, probably because most of the traffic shuffles on past its turnoff heading for Prairie Lakes. This hike in the unsung but rugged Smoky Mountains features a waterfall, two lovely meadows, a lake surrounded by high peaks, and a herd of mountain goats. I saw seven 400 yards above the lake. The shallow lake winterkills, but when it is restocked its fish grow fast on an abundance of shrimp.

Follow directions in trail No. 21 to reach the trailhead from where you'll hike along the Prairie Creek Trail for 2.5 miles to a fork and sign stating Miner Canyon Trail, and go left across Prairie Creek's two channels.

Climb moderately for .1 mile crossing Miner Creek and climb very steeply without switchbacks through open woods and at .3 mile reach a point overlooking the creek and a 65-foot waterfall that splashes and foams away in a miniature chasm. The left ridge rises 2,300 feet very close and showing its green-grassed summit in certain light. Climb steeply for 200 yards and ease to level along the creek's flat right bank until at 3 miles you climb .3 mile steeply and then dip left across Miner Creek and a meadow at the foot of a 1800-foot cliff. Turn right across the meadow into scrub timber, climb a knoll, cross another meadow, knoll, meadow—all good camping places, for fallen timber chokes the lake's shore. Wind 40 yards through firs to it, turquoise blue with a rocky far shore and jagged peaks close and high on all sides.

Miner Lake

TRAIL
Creek
2.5
8800
9200
8600
9400
Miner
PACK
3.0
Canyon
Prairie
8000
PACK
8800
8400
10000
0 10400
9800
N
8800
9800
9605
8736
Norton
Peak
3.7
8556
Miner
Lake
8770
9000
Prairie Lakes
9556
9200
8701
9400
9600
8701
8800
9910
9107
Norton
Lakes

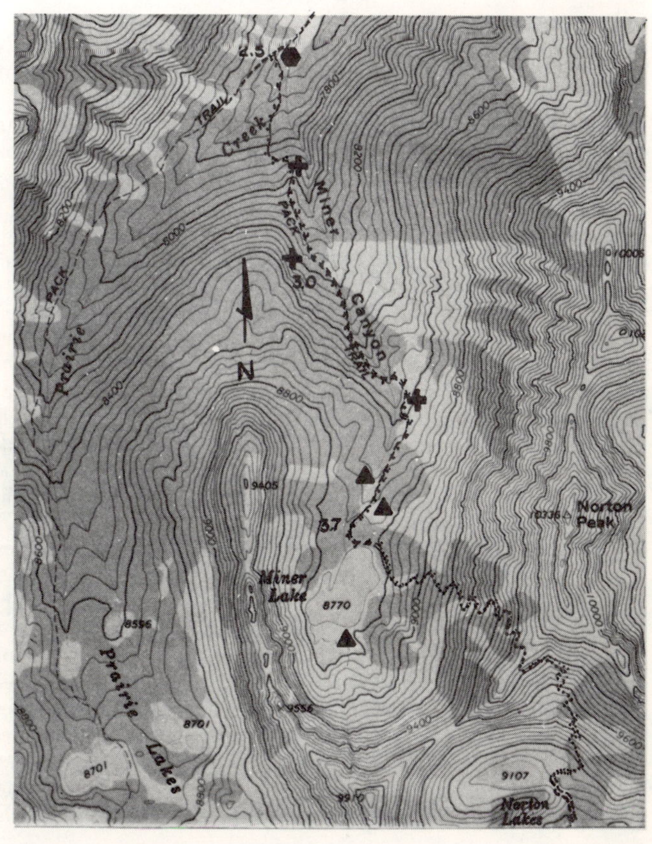

21 PRAIRIE LAKES

Distance: 4.6 miles
Elevation gain: 1,500 feet
High point: 8,701 feet
Allow 2.5 hours
Open late June through October
Topographic map:
U.S.G.S. Galena
7.5′ 1970

Hiking to Prairie Lakes takes one from dusty pine flats into a deep canyon bisected by a clear stream couched in green meadows, then up into spruce forest and, at the upper lakes, flower-spangled tundra. The creek is sparsely populated with rainbow trout in its lower reaches, and all trout should be released. Of the five lakes, only the lower holds trout, and since it usually winterkills, keeping the hatchery trout you catch won't hurt. Although this is a popular trail, the lake basin is two-tiered, and hilly, providing several secluded campsites and lots of room to explore. Goats roam the peaks above the lakes, and deer and coyotes are common. The excellent trail gains only 1500 feet, and is an excellent hike for those out of shape. At the 2-mile mark a short trail forks left to Miner Lake, and it, as well as Prairie Lakes, can all be visited in one day. An early start is suggested, as the middle portion of the trail crosses open ground.

Drive 18.3 miles north of Sun Valley and turn left at the Prairie Creek Road sign and drive 1 mile to a fork and bear right for 1.3 miles to another fork. Go right 0.3 mile to a sign stating West Fork Trail right, Prairie Cr. Lakes left. Drive a quarter mile beyond the sign to a registration box at the trailhead and park in the shade.

Climb gently in a traverse beside Prairie Creek splashing in waterfalls on your left through woods with a dry, rocky understory. Trees eliminate any view right; on the left rises a steep forested ridge. At 1.0 mile break into a meadow that in August is purple with lupine. Ahead is a jagged ridge enclosing the end of the valley. Across the meadow enter grassy woods, then cross a brace of sage-and-grass clearings to reach a sign at 2.3 miles stating Miner Lake left. Bear right climbing moderately for 0.2 mile to a clearing above which you see Norton Peak's nubbled rampart topping 10,000 feet.

Continue climbing moderately through woods to a clearing and the creek at 3.7 miles. Water stop! Climb steeply with the creek within either eye or earshot to an intricately sculptured cliff at 4 miles. Cross a large, lush meadow rimmed by spruce and fir, then leap the creek, and make 3 gentle switchbacks up a hill and drop gently to the lowest lake at 4.6 miles. Its far shore sweeps up from forest to grass to jagged ridgeline. Follow the trail left to the far shore and the inlet where there's camping space. To reach the upper lakes and more private camping follow the inlet up to the upper basin. By scaling the ridge to the west you'll obtain a great view of the crests of the Smokies.

Meadow, Upper Prairie Lakes Trail

Lower Prairie Lake

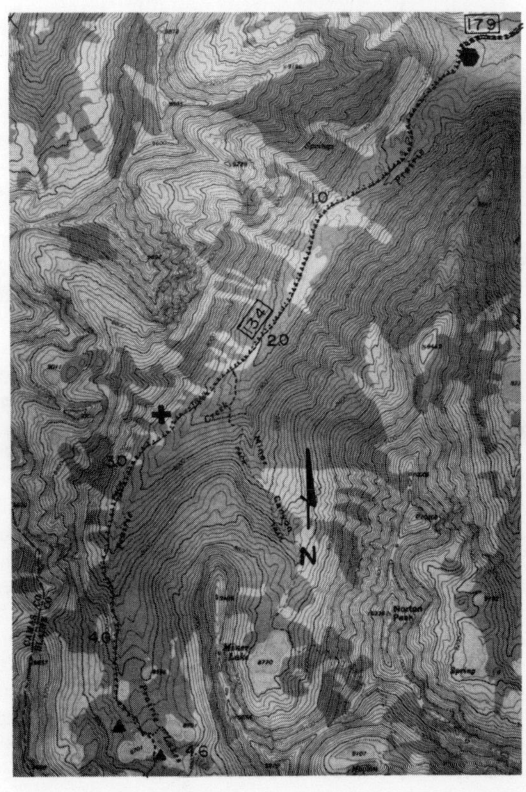

22   SNOWSLIDE LAKES

Distance: 7.2 miles
Elevation gain: 3,060 feet; loss: 1,680 feet
High point: 9,050 feet
Allow 5.5 hours
Open mid-June to November
Topographic map:
  U.S.G.S. Paradise Peak
  7.5′ 1970
  U.S.G.S. Frenchman Cr.
  7.5′ 1964

The jumble of ridges and peaks south of the Sawtooth Range and west of Sun Valley are loosely grouped under the name "Smoky Mountains." They are seldom visited by backpackers, although lovely meadows and lakes lie in cirques along their craggy 10,000-foot crests. Trout swim in the larger creeks, and goats and many mule deer graze the highest slopes all summer. The trails are narrow, the signs 1930 vintage. The trail to Snowslide Lakes traverses tilted parks dotted with spruce, descends to the Douglas fir canyon of Smoky Creek's north fork, turns up a beautiful unnamed creek of golden riffles, white waterfalls and blue pools to reach high meadows and crags and fishless but altogether lovely Snowslide Lakes.

Drive north from Sun Valley on U.S. 93 over Galena Summit to the Smiley Creek Store, cross Smiley Creek a few feet beyond, and take the first left turn, up Smiley Creek Road. Cross a cattleguard in .2 mile, ignore forks at .8, 2, and 3 miles. driving steadfastly ahead. Cross to Smiley Creek's right side at about 7 miles and immediately pass a fork going right to Vienna, but continue about another tenth-mile and park beside the road. The trail begins on the east side of the creek right where the 2 forks meet. It is faint at first but coalesces into a distinct track in a quarter-mile.

Traverse moderately to steeply beneath firs, making loops left uphill, crossing several brooks, the understory growing more lush for 1.3 miles to a small meadow. Skirt its left edge for a few feet, then cut right 90 degrees across it into timber. Veer left very steeply on a faint trace to an old double Forest Service blaze behind which is a rock bluff rooted in a huge block of granite. Cross another meadow below the bluff, enter woods and climb steeply left to a saddle at 1.8 miles. Walk left a few feet and view the southern Sawtooth peaks. South you look down into the wild, roadless canyons of Big Smoky Creek's headwaters. On the right a steep forest-and-meadow canyon wall culminates in a rocky summit holding tarns and meadows in a linked series of basins—summer range for large mule deer bucks.

Descend steeply about 450 yards along the ridge with a large tree-studded basin on the right, then veer left off the ridge, descending steeply across small flowered parks at the head of a yawning spruce and fir-covered U-shaped valley, easing to a moderate grade at 2.7 miles across meadows allowing a view of forested ridges on both sides splotched with smooth grassy parks. Abruptly descend steeply in forest for .4 mile only to resume an erratic descent with the creek in earshot on the right to a fork at 4.6 miles at the mouth of a canyon on the right. There is no sign to mark the fork, so watch for a flat on the right where the creek is invisible, and on the left a tall, lone lodgepole with a long split in its trunk showing the rust-colored core.

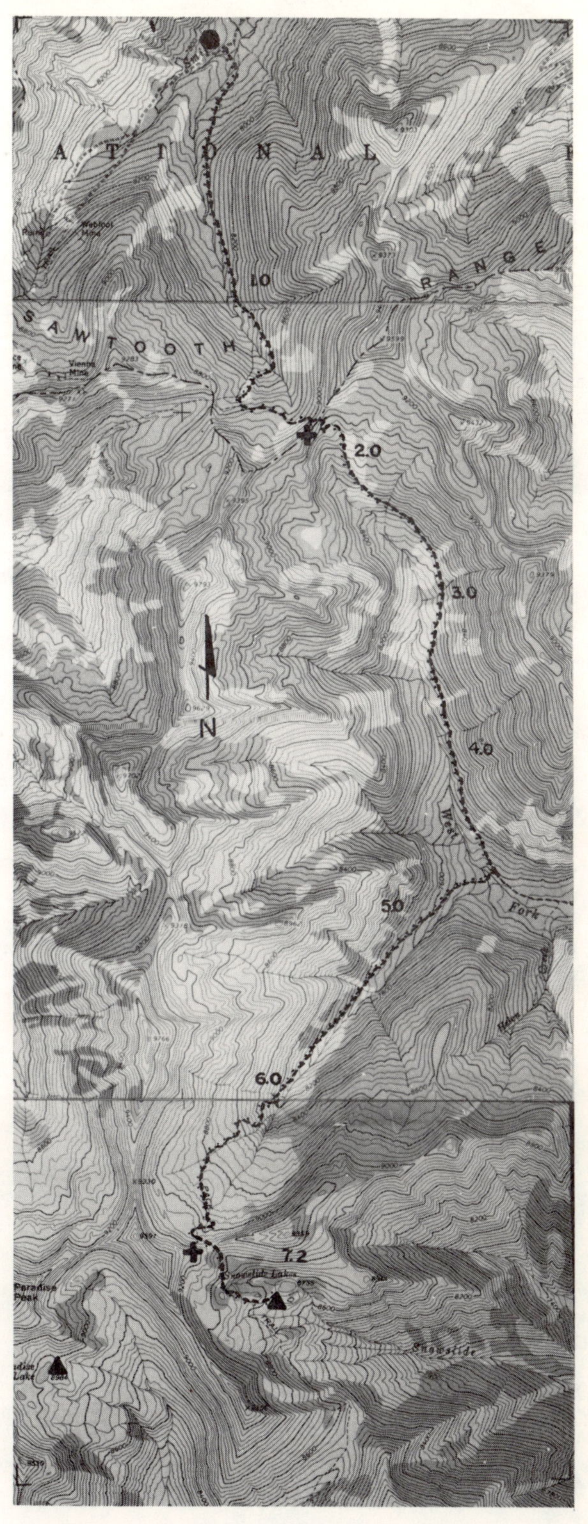

SAWTOOTH
ATIONAL
RANGE
Vienna Mine
Webfoot Mine
Paradise Peak
Snowslide Lake
1.0
2.0
3.0
4.0
5.0
6.0
7.2
N
West Fork

Lower Snowslide Trail

Walk right, watching for old blazes, and cross the creek, where the trail becomes distinct. Climb up the bank and veer sharply right across a park, then left into timber and traverse erratically along the canyon's right slope, the far slope also thickly timbered. The creek below flows through a corridor of willows, over golden-colored rock shallows between successive waterfalls. Cross 2 parks, then a third from which is visible a tall peak at the canyon's head. At 5.6 miles cross a rivulet, a rocky clearing, and enter an amphitheatre. Traverse a rock and sage slope and switchback steeply up to another basin, the sixth turn continuing left to cross the creek in its 15-foot gulley. A half-mile west the grass-and-spruce basin ends against the 9,500-foot ridge encircling it. Cross the creek and angle 45 degrees right from its direction, heading for that low saddle on the left side of the basin. In .2 mile climb steeply for 250 yards on a well-defined trail to a sign on the saddle stating Snowslide-Paradise Creek right. Descend steeply 300 yards to the first lake, really just a pond. The larger one lies just below and left of it, a green gem on a shelf whose lip curls up, cupping the lake. The canyon plunges down from the lake several hundred feet. In '77 it was fishless.

An easy hike by trail to the west takes you to Paradise Lake. If you've brought binoculars, be up early and glass for deer feeding in the meadows just below the rock cliffs. We spotted 3 trophy bucks.

Rainclouds over Snowslide Lake and Smoky Mountains

23 CHAMPION LAKES

Distance: 2.8 miles
Elevation gain: 1,400 feet; loss: 1,120 feet
High point: 9,780 feet
Allow 2.5 hours
Open late June to mid-October
Topographic map:
  U.S.G.S. Horton Peak
  7.5′ 1970
  U.S.G.S. Washington Peak
  7.5′ 1964

This short but steep trail leads to a high ridge affording a sweeping view south of the Boulder Mountains and the wild, trailless canyons and basins of their north-facing slope. In the opposite direction you'll descend into Champion Lakes' basin, timbered with 4 lakes, two of them holding cutthroat trout to 20 inches. This is a good dawn-to-dusk hike, but strenuous and not for small children. An easier but longer trail can be reached by road from U.S. 93 and leads up Champion Creek.

Drive north from Sun Valley over Galena summit and turn right a half-mile before reaching Smiley Creek Store at the Pole Creek Road sign. Drive 2 miles on gravel to a fork and bear right for Germania Basin. Ignore a sign at 5 miles reading "Champion Creek" and continue on the main road to another fork at 6 miles, and bear right, then left at another fork a mile ahead. On a narrow, twisting track pass Pole Creek summit's sign at 10 miles and descend another 1.2 to a Champion Creek Trail 105 sign on the left berm. Pull in and park in the shade, then walk 400 yards uphill to a registration box where the trail begins.

Angle 45 degrees from the box, crossing a rivulet, then turn right and climb steeply parallel to its 60-foot wide gulley, crossing it several times. At .5 miles ease to a moderate gradient for .2 mile and turn 90 degrees right and climb steeply without switchbacks through scattered pines and grass-brightened sage for .3 mile and make 4 short, very steep switchbacks. After another very steep stretch angle left to a summit at 1.4 miles.

Begin descending angling left very steeply for 130 yards, then right straight downhill, and again left into a grove of firs. Climb moderately up a low, sparsely timbered knoll and follow blazes down through woods to the lake's shore at 2.8 miles.

There are good campsites along the lake's upper end near the inlet, and many more down the valley around the other lakes. Waders are advised for fly fishermen who'll find trout close in to shore.

Champion Lakes

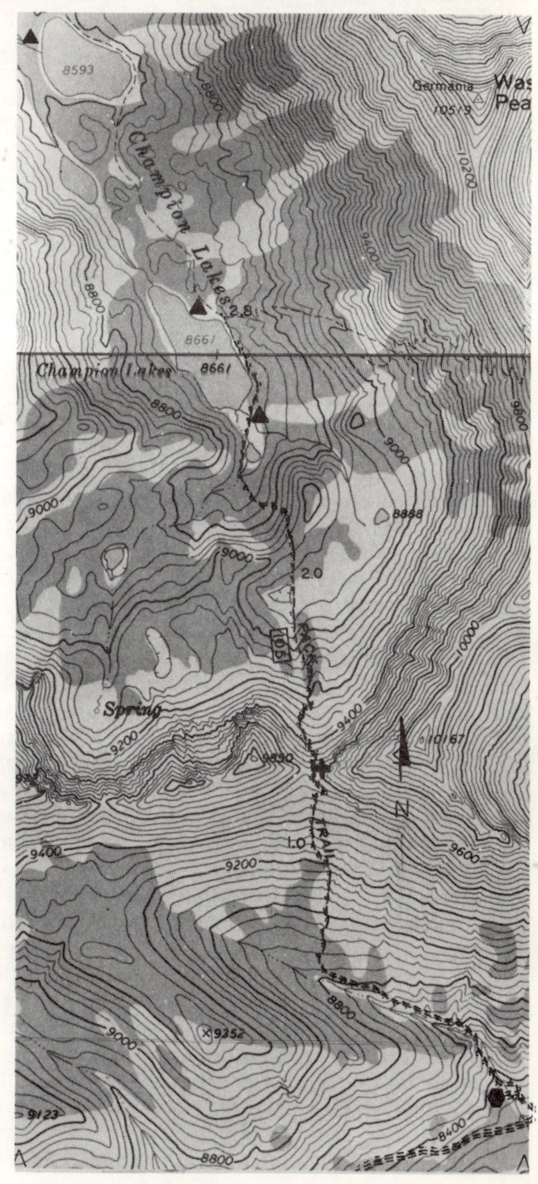

24 CHAMBERLAIN BASIN

Distance: 6 miles
Elevation gain: 1,950 feet; loss: 585 feet
High point: 9,780 feet
Allow 4 hours
Open July to mid-October
Topographic map:
  U.S.G.S. Galena
  7.5′ 1970
  U.S.G.S. Boulder Chain Lks.
  7.5′ 1964

Chamberlain Basin is a large, high, rolling alpine valley dotted with 8 lakes and ringed about by jagged mountains, including the range's highest, 11,820-foot Castle Peak, a sheer rock face eroded with parapets and towers, where your hair reportedly stands on end as thunderstorms approach. Mountain goats are everywhere, deer are common, and trout swim in the cold lakes. And there is enough room here that one can camp and never meet another person even if there were 20 in the valley. The long, tough hike runs a gamut of mountain terrain from creek-hugging, shaded traverses to dense timber to lush flower-sprinkled glades. Some impressive views of the wild north slope of the Boulder Mountains are had too. There are 2 other trails to Chamberlain, one from the road's end up 4th of July Creek, the other up Little Boulder Creek, but this one is the shortest.

Drive as you did for Champion Lakes No. 23, but continue past the Champion Lakes sign approximately 2 miles further, crossing Germania Creek twice. This section of the road is impassable to all but high-clearance or 4-wheel drive vehicles. About 600 yards after the second creek crossing where the road turns sharply left uphill there is a sign

stating Steep and Narrow Road, and to its right another: Three Cabins Trail to Bowery. Park here and pick up the trail behind the sign.

Hike gently downhill along the creek's left bank through hills close on both sides and heavily forested, blocking any view to the peaks above, the forest floor of grass and sage. The trail alternates between wooded glades and creek-side traverses till at .8 mile you loop left uphill around a promontory. Look right for a view up McRae Creek to snowy peaks, wild country with no trails. Descend moderately and cross Washington Creek at 1.3 miles and get a drink: there is no water ahead. Walk 80 feet to a fork and bear left in a long circle in the open to reach Washington Creek's bank further up and traverse it into gradually thickening woods to a fork at 2.5 miles and a sign banning motorized vehicles on the 3.3-mile trail going right to Chamberlain Basin, which you take.

Climb steeply for .9 mile in steep switchbacks to another fork and sign promising only 2.4 more miles if you turn right. 200 feet past the sign climb steeply for .2 mile along a south slope, then angle left .1 mile, and make 5 very steep switchbacks to a ridgetop at 3.9 miles. From here you can see 30 miles of Boulder and Pioneer Range peaks to the south. North, above the trees the rock scarp of Castle Peak is visible, creating a vivid contrast of brutal mammoth rock against soft needled treetops. Climb moderately for .5 mile through open woods and bare understory and make 2 steep switchbacks to the lip of the Basin at 4.6 miles.

Descend steeply .1 mile, then moderately across the rolling basin floor mostly open with scattered clumps of firs, then steeply down a hill to a lake at 5.6 miles. A few trophy cutthroats to 5 pounds lurk here, and can be taken on nymphs fished slowly along the bottom. Skirt the lake's shore and dip twice into meadows, then wind levelly through timber for .2 mile to the lower lake's shore hard by Castle Peak's base at 6.0 miles.

Campsites are along the inlet, where the trail to the upper lakes begins. They offer better fishing for cutthroats, and only lakes 2, 3, 7, and 8 contain trout. All can be fished from shore. To reach lakes at Little Boulder Creek's head take the trail from the lower lake east over a pass—about a 2-hour hike.

Chamberlain Lake

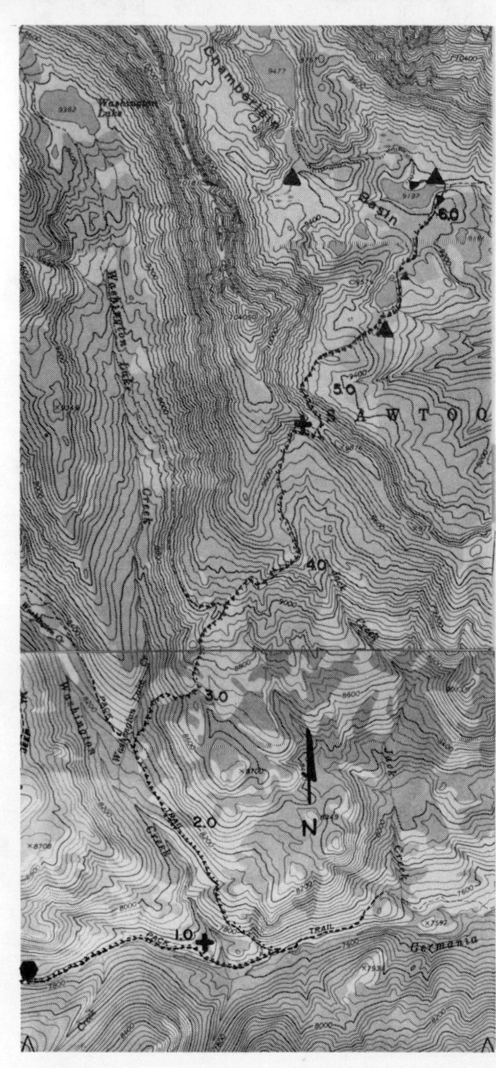

25 FOURTH OF JULY LAKE

Distance: 1.2 miles
Elevation gain: 525 feet
High point: 9,365 feet
Allow 45 minutes
Open July through October
Topographic map:
  U.S.G.S. Washington Peak
  7.5′ 1964

Lying at the foot of 10,882-foot Patterson Peak, this lake offers an easy hike that seems to belie the altogether lovely lake—but that's what it is, clean, cold, bordered by grass and flowers. Relax while gazing up at a stunning mountain where I saw two goats last September. A person using 4th of July as a bsae can make trips to Born, Washington, and Chamberlain Lakes, and catch trout for dinner in all three, while taking photos of goats and three mountain ranges.

Drive 9 miles north from Smiley Creek Store on U.S. 93 and turn right at the sign stating Fourth of July Creek. In one mile go left at a fork, and drive over a rough, tortuous road that is reported to be a tank trap to keep the Russians from crossing here on their way to savage Stanley and Salmon, and after 9 miles park by an old mining building at 4th of July Mine. There is a registration box near the creek and an area map.

Immediately cross 4th of July Creek and climb steeply for .1 mile through woods, then cross meadow sparsely studded with timber. The valley is wide on your left, the creek falling cleanly sparkling through its willow corridor. The opposite ridge's pines and firs thin near the top to a white 10,000-foot peak named after a black miner, a Mr. Blackman who ran the mine here for many years. Ahead you can already see the square but uneven bulk of Patterson Peak. At .5 miles keep right at a fork, climbing in shade till at .8 mile you climb steeply for .2 mile, then descend gently for another .2 mile to the lake's shore.

Shaded campsites in the trees on your left give a view of the lake and Patterson Peak's goats. This lake is heavily fished, and if you wish fish for dinner, hike a half mile further and descend to Washington Lake which has plenty of trout.

Fourth of July Lake below Patterson Peak

Unnamed peak on Fourth of July Trail

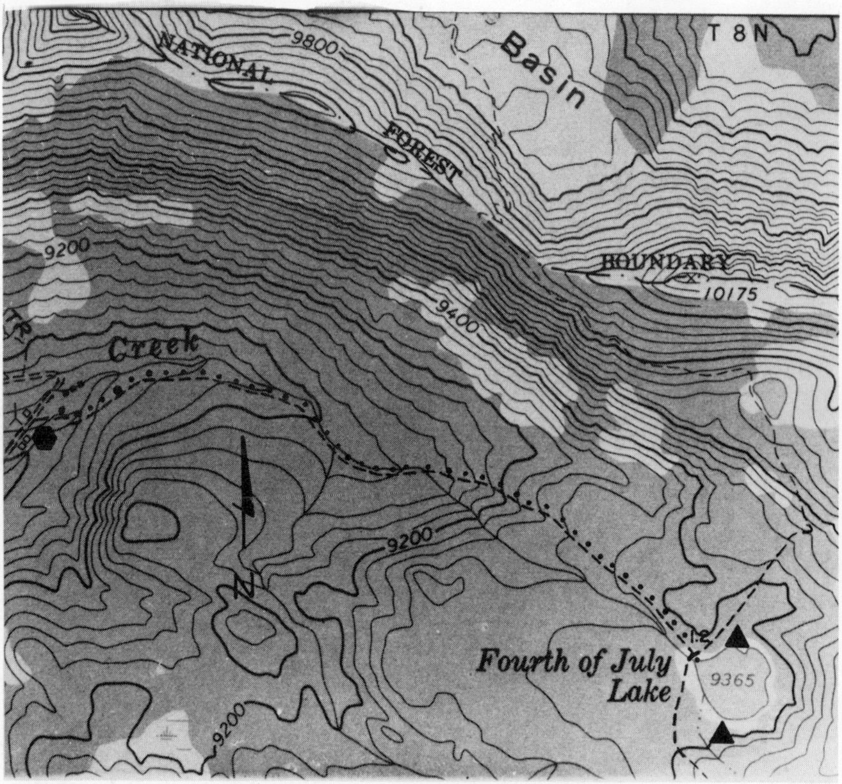

26 WASHINGTON LAKE

Distance: 2.1 miles
Elevation gain: 745 feet; loss: 225 feet
High point: 9,590 feet
Allow 1.5 hours
Open July through October
Topographic map:
  U.S.G.S. Washington Peak
  7.5′   1964
  U.S.G.S. Boulder Chain Lks.
  7.5′   1964

Washington Lake is a mellow hike, packed with exceptional scenery after a minimum of exertion. One has the impression of receiving a prize, a bonus, for in two easy miles you will pass 4 peaks approaching 11,000 feet, alpine lakes in a meadow, play tag with a meandering brook whose waters eventually reach the mighty Columbia, and receive the exhilaration, and piquant shout of the thousands of red and blue wildflowers. And probably, if your scan of Patterson peak turns up no mule deer, see shaggy white Rocky Mountain Goats. That's only the first half. Then you drop over a pass into a wide valley and big Washington Lake and search for a campsite while brook trout rise in its fertile waters. If you are agile and young you can clamber up the rock wall across the lake and look into Chamberlain Basin for a stunning view of the Lord of the Whiteclouds, Castle Peak, and the necklace of lakes at its foot. Resist, however, the urge to descend what appears to be a negotiable slope, be-

cause you will never make it back up. Instead, continue down Washington Creek to intersect another trail that will take you safely into the basin.

Since this hike is mostly in sunshine, plan your trip for early or late in the day. Follow directions in trail No. 25 to 4th of July Lake. With it in sight, the trail forks at 1.2 miles and you go right across a level meadow for .1 mile, then climb moderately through sparse timber and grass, then up a steep pitch at 1.8 miles, passing the rock-rubble shoulder of a huge peak on your right. This is a good place to begin a climb up its walk-up side for a view over the entire White Cloud Range.

Ahead now you can see Washington Lake. Descend moderately with one short, steep pitch for .2 mile and reach the lake. There is sheltered camping on the elevated ground near the outlet. Fly fishermen have 2/3 of the shoreline bare for backcasts, and trout are found all along the shore.

Washington Lake

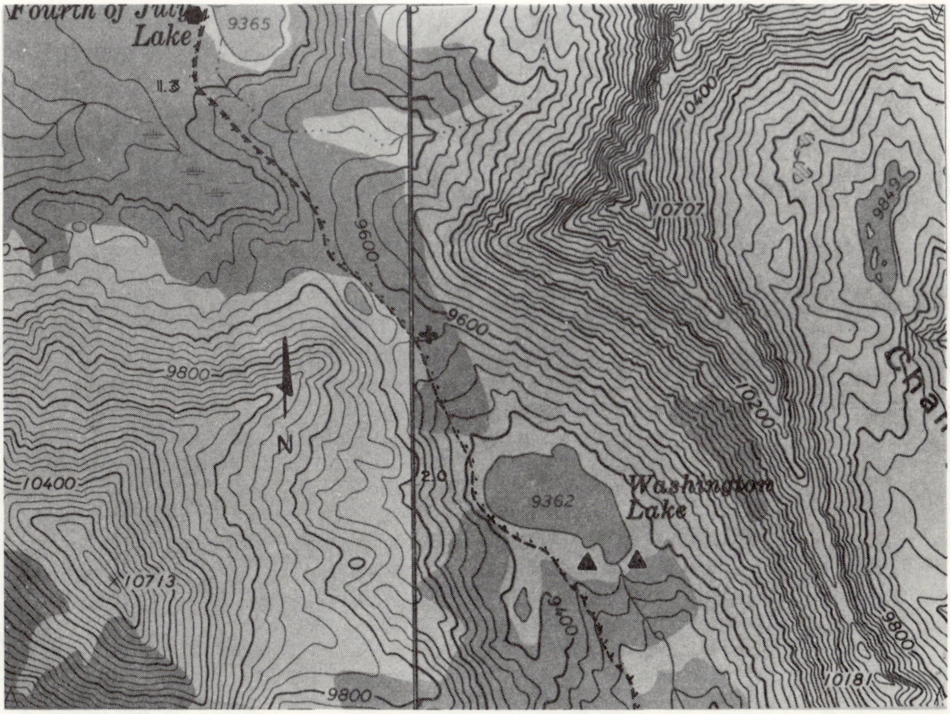

27 BORN LAKES

Distance: 3.7 miles
Elevation gain: 550 feet; loss: 600 feet
High point: 9,920 feet
Allow 3 hours
Open July to mid-October
Topographic map:
  U.S.G.S. Washington Peak
  7.5′ 1964
  U.S.G.S. Boulder Chain Lks.
  7.5′ 1964

These five little lakes are seldom visited even though they comprise a fairy kingdom of terraced meadows separating five blue lakes tucked at the base of ragged crags on a seemingly inaccessible shelf, over whose edge plunges a thin waterfall: a fortress for one of J. R. R. Tolkien's mythical Hobbit kings? No, their pristine condition results from the last half of the trail existing but intermittently, and by their being hidden by trees even though the trail's legible first half ends at an overlook 400 feet above them. None of the lakes can be seen from any of the others, so as you follow their interlaced out- and inlets (which provide fair spawning grounds for their native cutthroats) you have a delightful childish sense of surprise and exploration. Mountain goats graze almost to the lakes' shores. Though outdoorsmen baptized in cross-country travel will have no difficulty finding the lakes, hikers who have never left a trail's security can make the big leap now, for you'll definitely reach the lakes safely, but it will require effort, and therefore give practice, in keeping your bearings.

Drive as you did for trail No. 25 and at the trail fork and sign at 1.2 miles go left to the edge of 4th of July Lake. Eventually you will top that ridge on the left, then drop down its far side and hike 2 more miles to the lakes. For now, follow the left fork on around the lake shore for about 180 paces to a rivulet. The trail is faint in places here. Cross it and reach a second trickle and walk up it about 75 paces, then angle 45 degrees right across that flat meadow on the right, aiming for a stone cairn on its far edge which may not be there next year, which is .2 mile from the trail fork and 1.4 from your car.

Climb from the cairn on a plain trail for 200 yards, then switchback moderately with one short descent through the reddish-brown trunks of old whitebark pines to a saddle at 2.1 miles. Look west to the Sawtooth Valley and Range, and east across a vast canyon to the white limestone peaks of the White Clouds, with Alabaster Peak directly across from you. Below is a wide, rolling, grassy bench rampant with wildflowers. It falls off 700 feet into Warm Springs Creek's canyon. But where are Born Lakes? Look right, at the head of the valley, slightly left and at the foot of Patterson Peak, and you'll see a tilted, rough plateau at the upper limit of trees, where the lakes nestle.

Go left along the saddle 180 yards, then angle right where there was no sign in '77 onto a very distinct trail and descend steeply in 5 switchbacks to the bench where the trail ends. Continue on at the angle of the last trail segment across spongy grass and heather to the uppermost scrub conifers at the bench's rim at 2.7 miles. Below and right is a rockslide flowing downhill left. Descend steeply from the rim along the rockslide's edge for about 60 yards. Several faint trails made by hikers hint at routes across the slide. Carefully traverse across the slide's lower third to the distant timber about .6 miles where you'll stay between the trees on the left and the cliffs on the right for another .4 mile to reach the first lake at 3.7 miles. Using the map, you can easily locate the other lakes by following outlet creeks to them.

Campsites are everywhere. The naturally reproducing population of cutthroats aren't difficult to catch, and eating a couple will make a healthy dent in the slightly crowded situation. But no more than 2, ya hear?

Born Lake No. 2

Looking towards Alabaster Mountain across Ants Basin, Born Lakes Trail

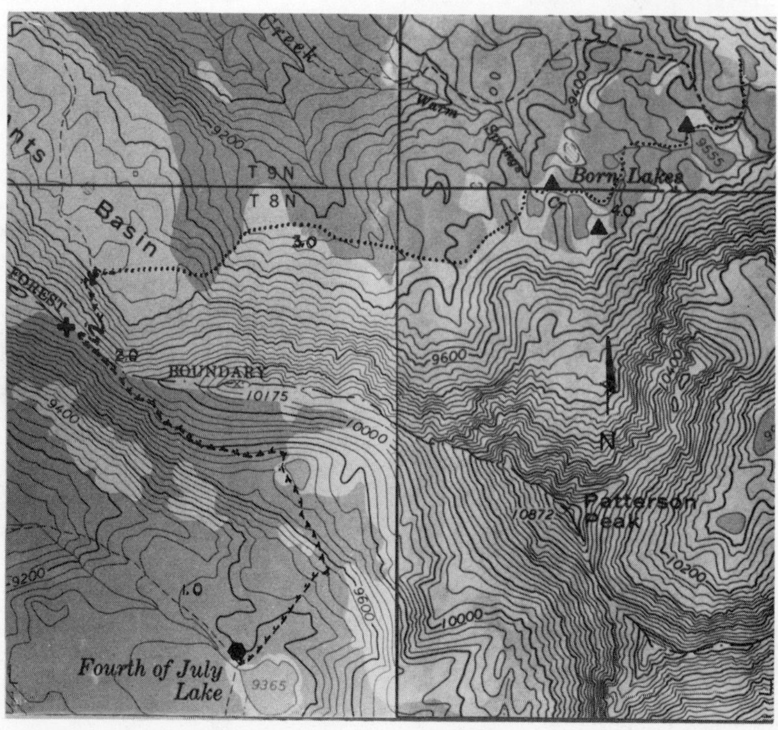

28 CASINO CREEK

Distance: 6.2 miles
Elevation gain: 1,300 feet
High point: 8,620 feet
Allow 3.5 hours
Open early June through October
Topographic map:
  U.S.G.S. Casino Lakes
  7.5′   1963

If it's possible for a homesick New Englander to find a brook trout pond complete with Catskills topography out west, Lower Casino Lake is the place. The trail doesn't intimidate one with awesome vistas and lordly crags, instead winding like an Appalachian trace through pine woods its entire length to finally reach a lily-padded pond brimming with *Salvilinus fontinallus* to 14''. The author caught 12 trout in 14 casts, and the lake's Eastern Brook Trout can use more pressure to balance their reproducing population.

But the trail isn't easy, gaining 1,300 feet in a steady grade with few switchbacks. With six other lakes nearby in the low, wooded terrain and few hikers, this is an ideal place for a family with small children to spend a week. Drop over the ridge and angle west to Rough Lake, or south to Garland Lakes. Deer summer here, grazing in the meadow below the lower lake, where flowers are profuse.

From Stanley drive north on U.S. 93 about 4.7 miles and turn right at a presently unsigned bridge across the Salmon River and turn right again and in 600 yards cross Casino Creek. 80 yards beyond at the Big Casino Creek Trail sign on the left park under trees on the right.

An alternate trail climbs from Boundary Creek near U.S. 93 south of Stanley, crosses a high ridge and descends past the upper lake to lower Casino Lake. It affords spectacular views of the Sawtooth Mountains and Redfish Lake. It is a steep, dry trail, with water available only near the top. By arranging an auto ferry or hitchhiking the 11 miles between both Casino and Boundary trailheads, a loop trip, up Casino Creek and down this trail, is possible. To reach the Boundary trailhead, drive 5.3 miles south of Stanley across the first Salmon River bridge, and .6 mile further turn left onto a dirt track that passes a Fish and Game Dept. cabin on the right and reaches a registration box and the trailhead. Begin this hike early and carry water; it's available only near the top.

Walk on a road .2 mile to a fork and bear right and climb gently along the creek's right bank for 1 mile to a clearing at the road's end. Cross the creek's gulley to the left and intersect the trail following the left bank. You are 120 yards left of the creek. Climb gently through sage, viewing a low timbered valley ahead. Pass two sets of beaver ponds at .7 mile and enter lodgepole woods and grass with the creek about 50 yards to the right. Traverse moderately left into sagebrush at 1.2 and climb steeply straight uphill beside the trail that is a gravel trough for .4 mile and ease to a moderate grade with occasional steep pitches in dense woods to an icy rivulet at 3.4 miles. After a drink resume climbing erratically and in a gentle glade at 4.3 miles cross to the right bank, climb very steeply for .1 across a bog, loop steeply twice uphill right, and descend and cross to the left bank, then after a steep pitch to the right at 5 miles.

Now climb moderately away from the creek for 400 yards then jog left across it again, climb steeply for .2 mile and recross to the right bank. Now ease to moderate grade entering a broad, sparsely tree-studded basin with a huge meadow on your left. Angle left at 5.8 up a steep pitch then down to the lower lake at 6 miles. By continuing on the trail you'll reach the second lake, a frog pond, in a mile. By switchbacking above it to the ridge and then taking a faint trail right along the basin rim you'll reach the upper lake and its small brook trout. From this same ridge a left turn and subsequent contouring around the mountain will take you to Rough Lake, also good fishing. Hiking straight ahead, according to a sign, will take you to Garland lakes in 2 miles. There is excellent camping around the lower lake's west shore and in the meadow below it. The middle lake is brushy, but the upper one is nice and receives first light in the morning. The lakes can be fished from shore.

Angler at Lower Casino Lake

Parkland along Lower Casino Lake

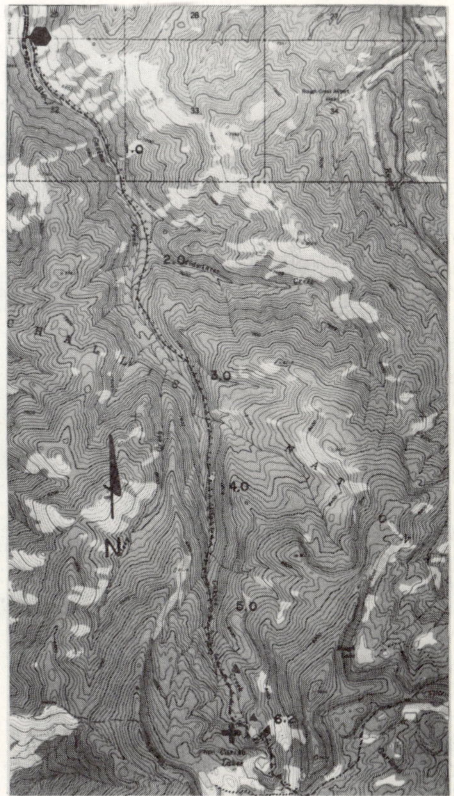

29 WALKER LAKE

Distance: 6.3 miles
Elevation gain: 1,460 feet
High point: 9,240 feet
Allow 4 hours
Open late June to late October
Topographic map:
 U.S.G.S. Boulder Chain Lks.
 7.5′ 1964

This popular trail, uncrowded after Labor Day, offers a scenic entrance to the White Cloud Range at an easy gradient through close woods-and-meadow scenery, with many campsites along the way in view of snow-splotched peaks. Tree-lined Walker Lake is asplash with rainbow trout, and is a gateway to higher tundra country accessible by the Island Lake Trail branching off left below Walker, and by the route from Walker's west end that switchbacks up to Big Boulder Basin. From Island and Big Boulder miles of cross-country hiking in meadowland unfolds, with several unnamed lakes providing exquisite campsites.

Follow directions in trail No. 30 and at the sign and trail fork at 1.7 miles stating Walker Lake 5 Miles, go right. The trail is suddenly narrow because cycles are banned. Cross Big Boulder Creek on logs, climb a steep pitch away from the creek across a sage hillside, gaining altitude above the wide, forested valley with high peaks making the opposite side. At 2 miles top a ridge, then climb moderately through 3 groves of trees, and descend to a lovely meadow at 2.6 miles. Immediately climb steeply right from the meadow for 100 yards, then undulate moderately across an old burn for .7 mile to the rim of a 200-foot deep chasm cut by Boulder Creek. There's good fishing for cutthroats in its pools. Quickly descend to another large meadow with a spectacular reddish mountain close on its far side. Cross the creek and turn left to parallel it for about 100 yards, cross another one, and at the sign Quicksand Meadows veer 90 degrees right to enter woods at 3.6 miles. Wind .2 miles to the creek and fork and go left 80 feet to cross the creek on logs. A short distance ahead recross the creek on logs again and climb in 4 moderate switchbacks, then turn left and parallel the creek through woods growing more dense and verdant. At 4.2 miles descend winding away from the creek 400 yards, then climb steeply right to a wide, thinly flowing waterfall in the trees on the left. Angle steeply left, crossing 2 small creeks at 5 miles, up 2 more steep pitches, then level to a fork and sign, Island Lake left, Walker Lake right 1 Mile. Climb a short, steep pitch and descend into a vale with a lovely placid meadow stream teeming with small trout. The trail seems to end at the creek; wade to the other side and find the trail curving left, then up to a granite shelf, then through thick woods 150 yards to the lake shore at 6.3 miles.

Best campsites are near the outlet and at the west end. Flat ground is scarce along the north shore. Walker is over-populated with rainbows to 9 inches, so please take your limit. Trout are found all along the shore. To reach Big Boulder Lakes follow the trail to the inlet, where it ends. Several traces wind up through the woods along the inlet; the most legible starts directly across the creek from where the trail ends. You'll lose it several times in the mile you'll follow it, but the important part not to miss is the switchbacks. Follow it to an amphitheatre, where the cascading creek suddenly levels in a meadow and begins meandering. Immediately go 90 degrees left from the creek and find the trail zig-zagging up to the upper basin. If you miss them you'll have a tough time safely scaling the rock wall forming the basin. Big Boulder Lakes have rainbow and cutthroat trout to 3 pounds.

*Hikers crossing old burn,
Walker Lake Trail*

*Angler on Big Boulder Creek,
Walker Lake Trail*

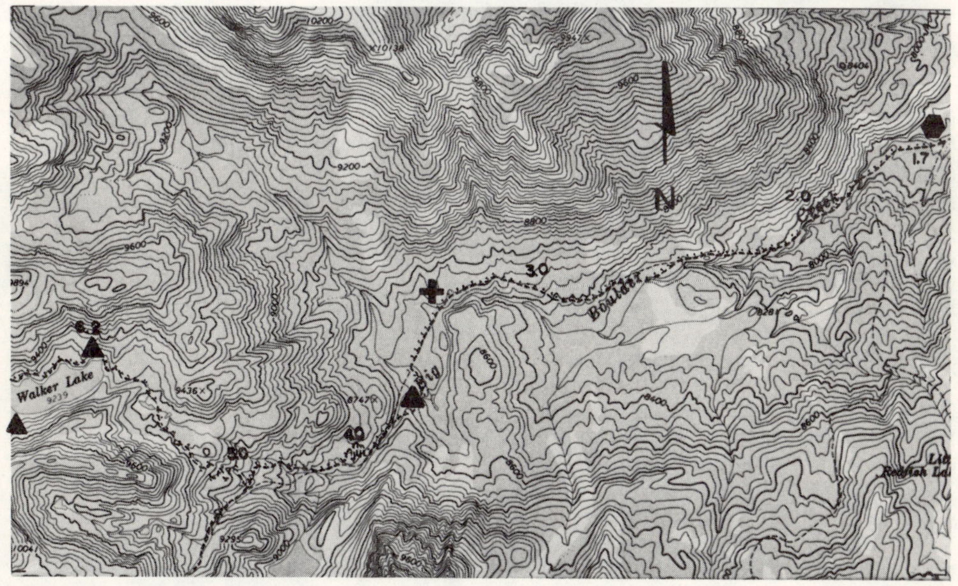

30 FROG LAKE TRAIL

Distance: 7.8 miles
Elevation gain: 2,360 feet; loss: 1,725 feet
High point: 9,580 feet
Allow 5 hours
Open late June to November
Topographic map:
  U.S.G.S. Livingston Cr.
  7.5′   1964
  U.S.G.S. Boulder Chain Lks.
  7.5′   1964

This wide, popular and spectacular trail of moderate gradient terminates in the stunning valley of Little Boulder Creek, where photographers find the classic view of Castle Peak that has graced a score of major publications including *Life.* A continuous panorama of 11,000-foot peaks unfolds along the way, and one never lacks for shade or water except descending to Frog Lakes, two blue trout factories with excellent camping and only a mile from a canyon holding the 11 Boulder Chain Lakes. From Frog it's a 7-mile hike to Chamberlain Basin and its lakes, passing on the way spur trails to Castle and other lakes. Since the Frog Lake trail is open to cycles, a 3-day trip allowing for one of these additional hikes is advised if you're after solitude. Being graded for cycles, this is an excellent hike for anyone in poor health who still wants to truck, but is a bit long for children under 12 years. As with most major trails in the White Clouds, this one is uncrowded after Labor Day.

Drive about 3.5 miles east of Clayton on U.S. 93 and turn right at a sign stating East Fork Salmon River Road and in approx. 11 miles cross Big Boulder Creek and in 60 yards a road forking right with no sign but which you take. Follow the single dirt track 5 miles to a fork and sign stating Railroad Ridge right, Castle Peak trail left. In 300 yards turn 90 degrees left driving through the Livingston Mine property and park next to a rail fence at the left of a sign reading Livingston Mill-Castle Peak Trail.

From the registration box climb steeply on a thoroughfare for 150 yards, make sharp left and right turns, then ease to a moderate grade, with the creek sporadically visible on the left, thick forest on the right, and striking reddish canyon walls on the left. At 1 mile cross a bridge to Boulder Creek's right bank and suddenly see ahead an A-shaped snowy peak. Walk on the level through lodgepoles to a fork and sign just beyond a cold stream at 1.7 miles stating Frog Lake left 6 miles. The trail will be gentle with moderate pitches from here to the lakes.

Climb undulating and winding in timber but frequently traversing a ridge from which the high, white peaks above Walker Lake are visible across a vast, forested valley below. The long white peak sloping down from left to right is dubbed by locals Alabaster Peak. At 2.9 miles reach a small sign on the left stating Little Redfish Lake 1 mile. It offers excellent camping and fishing for 12-inch cutthroat trout, but limit your catch from this non-reproducing population. Fir and spruce are taking over from pines here, and grassy, flowered clearings are everywhere as you continue switchbacking across bridged rivulets. At 5.5 miles level out and wind across a whitebark and spruce flat, passing a pond on the left, then making 5 moderate switchbacks that take you to the summit at 6.2 miles. The snowy crown of Castle Peak shows above closer peaks to the southwest, and south are the distant blue peaks of the Pioneer Range. The ridge you're standing on curves up another 1500 feet, where you may see goats.

Descend in 7 switchbacks on a sparsely-timbered slope, also over-grazed, to a willow thicket, then enter a 150-yard corridor of trees and emerge on a grassy flat beside the lake at 7.8 miles.

Best camping is along the east shore. Both lakes hold cutthroat trout to 24 inches but you'll have to fish early and late to catch them. Otter Shrimp nymphs work well, in No. 14 or 16. If it's a limit of breakfast trout you desire hike a mile to Boulder Chain Lakes, where a surplus of rainbows provided by natural production means fishing pressure is beneficial.

Castle Peak from Frog Lake Trail

Frog Lakes from Trail

31 ALICE LAKE

Distance: 5.7 miles
Elevation gain: 1,600 feet
High point: 8,595 feet
Allow 3.5 hours
Open July through October
Topographic map:
  U.S.G.S. Snowyside Peak
  7.5′   1964

Hiking to Alice Lake fills one with wonder and a sense of adventure. The first half takes you deep into an alpine valley with sides so steep they elicit the sensation of being overhung, and up ahead maybe 6 miles distance you see jagged peaks below which you think Alice must lie. But then the trail goes right, scaling the canyon wall, leading you into a landscape of lush green vegetation and smooth white granite rock. The lake's jagged skyline is the epitome of the Spanish word "sierra," or saw, and just above this excellent brook trout fishery lie two smaller but as spectacular lakes. By continuing north over the pass above Twin Lakes you can make a loop down into Toxaway Lake, past Farley Lake, and over a ridge to Pettit Lake and your car. Though a toughie can make the trip in a day, a weekend or 3 days is recommended.

Drive 45 miles north from Sun Valley on U.S. 93 to a sign on the road's east berm announcing the Pettit Lake Access Road and turn west onto it. Drive 1 mile to a 3-way fork without a sign and turn right, crossing a creek, and at another fork turn left and in about half a mile reach a large campground and keep right to park near the registration box.

From the box wind and undulate along Pettit Lake's shore in and out of shade, passing a sign at .2 mile stating Alice Lake 5¾ miles. Across the lake McDonald Peak rises to a smooth, sharp point, and between trees you can see Pettit Creek's granite-walled valley Yosemite tries to copy. Keep left at the sign and at the lake's far end enter woods and climb gently winding through lush understory to the base of cliffs at 1.6 miles. Begin climbing moderately now, meeting Pettit Creek at a waterfall at 1.8, veering right to cliffs, then back to its left bank at 2.2 miles. Continue climbing erratically for .6 mile, then cross back right and enter a valley of scrub firs and aspen with McDonald's cliff-face with its goats on the left. Climb 1.3 miles in 4 moderate switchbacks in the hot sun and look back down at a huge old beaver pond, then east across the Sawtooth Valley to the White Cloud Range.

Make 6 switchbacks across a rockslide, scaling Pettit Creek's canyon wall, and reach a long cascade at 4.2 miles, switchback gently to cross a creek, and wind gently into a shallow hanging valley of conifers growing amid granite slabs. Cross to the creek's right bank and leave it, making 5 moderate switchbacks up a low ridge, then veering left across the creek at 4.8 miles. Climb erratically for .5 mile to a fork, the left going to a spear-shaped monolith 1,500 feet high dubbed El Capitan. Cross to the creek's right bank and meander another .4 mile through open woods and berry bushes, passing 2 small lakes to quite suddenly reach the lake at 5.7 miles. At its far end are 8 serrated peaks blotched with snowfields.

To have secluded camping cross to the lake's south shore here and find flat spots all along it. Good camping spots abound along the north shore but so do campers. Alice's brookies reach 11 inches and are easy to catch until mid-August, when they begin feeding mostly in the evening on midges. Natural reproduction is excellent, and a limit of the pink-fleshed beauties should cause no twinge of conscience. To reach Twin Lakes and their excellent fishing walk to Alice's west end where the sign marks the easy 1-mile ascent. If you've planned no loop but climb to Twin Lakes for the view, it's well worth it to continue up to the pass for a nonpareil photo of the two and the peaks above them.

Alice Lake

Thunderclouds over Twin Lake, above Alice Lake

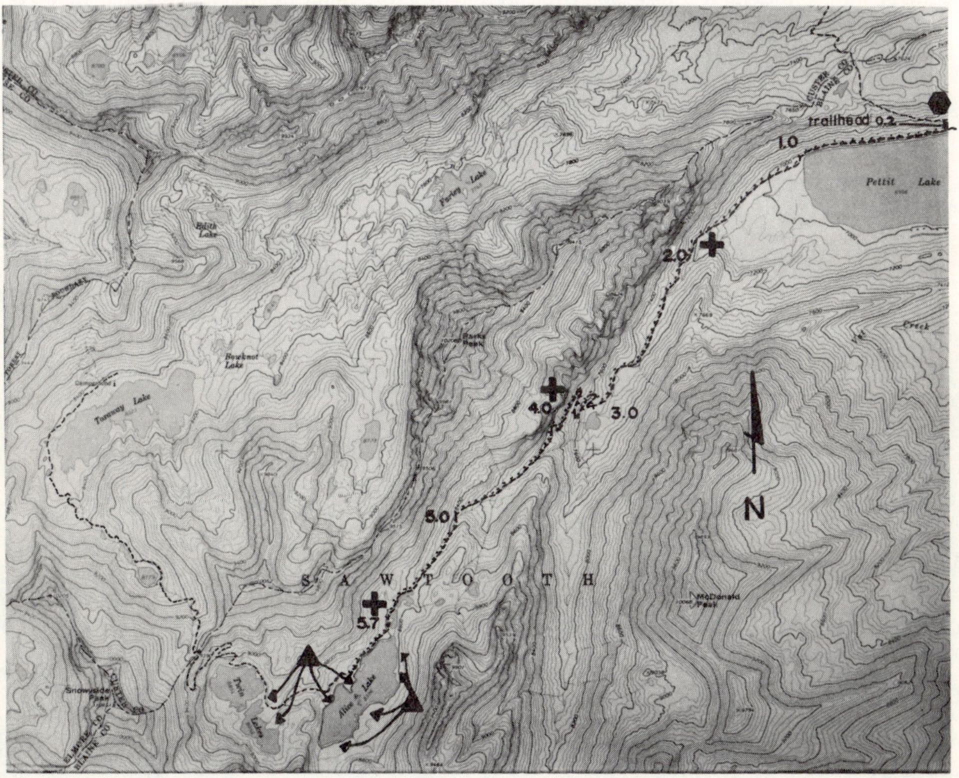

32   TOXAWAY LAKE

Distance: 7.3 miles
Elevation gain: 1,325 feet
High point: 8,325 feet
Allow 4 hours
Open July through October
Topographic map:
  U.S.G.S. Snowyside Peak
  7.5′ 1964

Like all the spectacular Sawtooth trails this one should be hiked in September when the crowds have dispersed. Also typical of the range's eastern slope, this one features a canyon, cliffs, soaring peaks, and 2 beautiful lakes. The lower lake, Farley, is itself worth the hike, with good brook trout fishing, and camping in a stunning setting. A tough 2 and comfortable 3-day loop trip can be made by continuing past Toxaway Lake over a 9,000-foot pass below Snowyside Peak to Twin Lakes, then down to Alice Lake and back to your car at Pettit. Total distance is about 17 miles. Or, if you have more time, backtrack from Toxaway to the Edith Lake cutoff, then drop down to Imogene Lake, then to Hell Roaring Lake, and take the Alpine Way Trail south to Yellowbelly Lake and over the hill to your car.

Follow directions in trail No. 31 to Tin Cup Transfer Camp, and from the registration box hike 1 mile to a sign indicating Toxaway Lake 7 miles right. Switchback moderately with frequent steep pitches through grass and sage with scattered firs for shade and reach a ridgetop at 1 mile. Look back at Pettit Lake and above it you can see the steep-walled valley of upper Pettit Creek and the jagged crags above Alice Lake. Descend in erratic switchbacks through woods with a dead log-and-pine needle understory to a fork at 1.7 miles and a sign pointing left to Toxaway Lake 5.5 miles.

Hike on the level valley floor through lodgepole forest for 1.2 miles then over a steep incline, and on to the creek at 2.8 miles, crystal water flowing over fine gravel—an ideal spawning stream for the rainbows and brook trout of Yellowbelly Lake. Cross to the right bank, make 2 switchbacks, and traverse along the bank to a steep pitch at 3.8 miles, cross a brook, and enter lush grass and brush forest floor. Soon meet Yellowbelly Creek again where it cascades through a 15-foot slot in granite. Angle steeply right from the creek around huge boulders fallen from the cliffs that oddly appear to be haphazardly glued together. At 4.4 miles the narrow valley opens into a bowl of grass and scrub conifers with the creek splashing down in a succession of pools, and above on the right a peak rising 2,000 feet.

Cross the bowl and climb moderately for .4 mile, passing a 145-foot waterfall, cross a footbridge at 4.9 miles and reach Farley Lake, a sparkling blue-black gem with an island in its center and beaucoup brook trout in its depths. Look back and see 30 miles away the White Cloud Peaks and Castle Peak. Up the valley are jagged peaks about 4 miles away. Beyond Farley Lake traverse moderately through scrub conifers and aspen to 2 switchbacks at 5.6 miles that take you into a higher, flatter valley, a hodge-podge of scrub timber, brush, meadow, and exposed granite. Undulate and twist for .3 mile, then climb steeply to a meadow and waterfall at 6 miles. Cross this creek and climb erratically but never steeply to a sign at 6.4 stating Edith Lake Trail right, a good lake to take children fishing because it is overpopulated with brook trout. Continue left past a small lake on the left at 6.8 miles, a scraggly meadow, a pond, a larger lake, and another meadow. Climb moderately now, crossing a wood log bridge, and quickly reach Toxaway Lake at 7.3 miles. It is dark blue and set in steep, pale granite flecked with sparkling mica, with an S-curve in its middle that lends it a fiord-like narrowness.

All along the shore trout fishing is excellent. By late August the reproducing brookies begin feeding only in the evening, and in September imitations of flying red (No. 16) and black (No. 12) ants are necessary to take these dusk risers. The flotsam of ants collects along the lee side of the lake, where the brookies to 11 inches congregate in a feeding frenzy. Camping is limited to widely-spaced sites along the north shore, with a few at the west end.

Storm clouds over the White Cloud Mountains from Toxaway Lake Trail

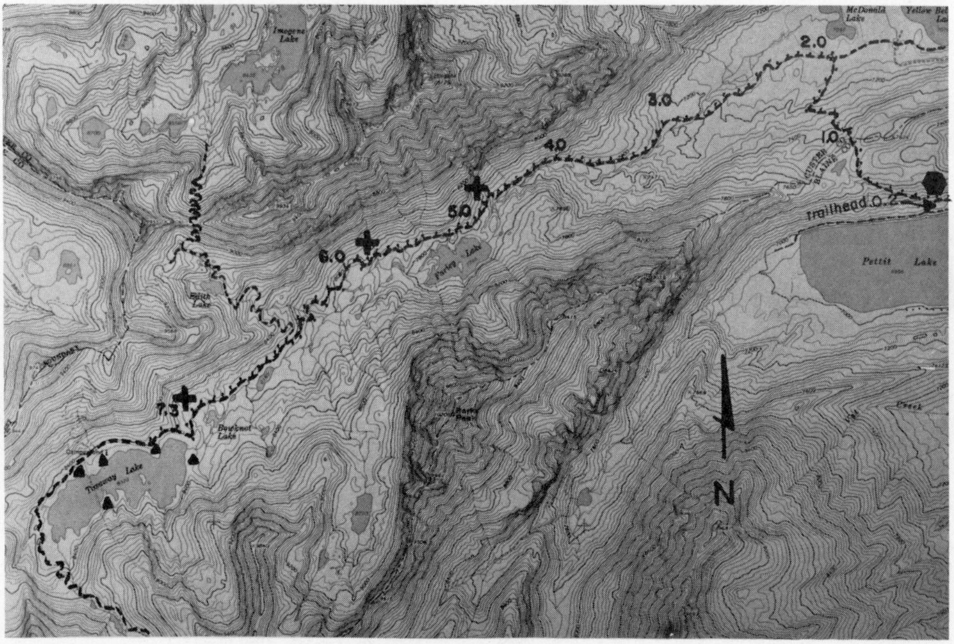

33 HELL ROARING AND IMOGENE LAKES

Distance: 6 miles
Elevation gain: 1,235 feet
High point: 8,436 feet
Allow 3.5 hours
Open July through October
Topographic map:
 U.S.G.S. Mt. Cramer
 7.5′ 1963

Though 1,000 feet separate them, these lakes are equally spectacular. The trail to Hell Roaring is mostly flat, the steep section going from its upper end to Imogene, where the summer temperatures will be cooler than below. If the stamina or age of a hiking group varied, this would be an ideal hike, some stopping at Hell Roaring after a couple gentle miles, while the hardier souls trucked on up to Imogene Lake, long and deep with a rockbound shore shipped intact from Maine to Idaho. A loop trip with breath-taking views of the multi-spined crest of the Sawtooth Range could be made by continuing from Imogene 4 miles to Toxaway Lake then east to Farley Lake and back to Hell Roaring Creek.

Drive 9 miles north from Smiley Creek on U.S. 93 and turn left immediately after passing the Fourth of July Creek Road sign at a sign stating Hell Roaring Lake and cross the Salmon River on a bridge and see a sign,

Hell Roaring Lake 5 Miles. If you're driving a modern low-clearance auto park and begin hiking here. If you've a VW or similar car turn left at this sign and follow the road to a fork, and go right to Hell Roaring Creek, grinding uphill over football-sized rocks and across marshy ground that is impassable in wet weather, and after 4 tortuous miles reach the road's end at the creek. There are numerous logging spurs off the main road so be alert.

From a sign stating Imogene Lake 5.9 Hell Roaring 1.8 cross the creek, a limpid, placid meadow stream here which offers fair rainbow and brook trout fishing for small, wary trout, and surmount a small ridge to a registration box at the intersection with the trail that began by the Salmon River Bridge. Climb gently through a broad, pine-forested valley, bearing right at a fork, past a creek and then a meadow at 1.7 miles, then up a moderate incline for .2 mile to Hell Roaring Lake, large with a massive peak at its upper end. Its small brook trout frequent most of the shoreline but congregate at the west end in mid-September.

Turn 90 degrees left across the creek on a bridge and skirt the south shore for a mile, then veer left and make 4 easy switchbacks in .4 mile. Hell Roaring Creek's rush can be heard somewhere off in the trees on the right, while on your left a jagged rock wall of the Sawtooth's front slope looms ahead. Traverse right 400 yards, then at 3.5 miles veer left across an avalanche path bristly with scrub conifers. High on the left is a saw-toothed ridge and along its base a horizontal snowfield with vertical fingers. Cross a creek at 4.3 miles and loop right, climbing moderately in forest, then through a defile and level out to wind gently in woods, passing a lily-padded pond and then a brook-trout lake on the right. Climb moderately here, crossing the creek and at 5.3 miles looping right around a park, then left across the creek by a waterfall, then straight to the lake at 6.0 miles.

Walk left around the lake to the west shore for camping. Glass for goats on the peaks. Climb the western ridge and look for untold miles across endless mountain ridges. The brook and cutthroat trout to 14 inches that feed along the south and eastern shores are difficult to reach if fly casters don't have waders because the trees along shore eat flies.

Hell Roaring Lake

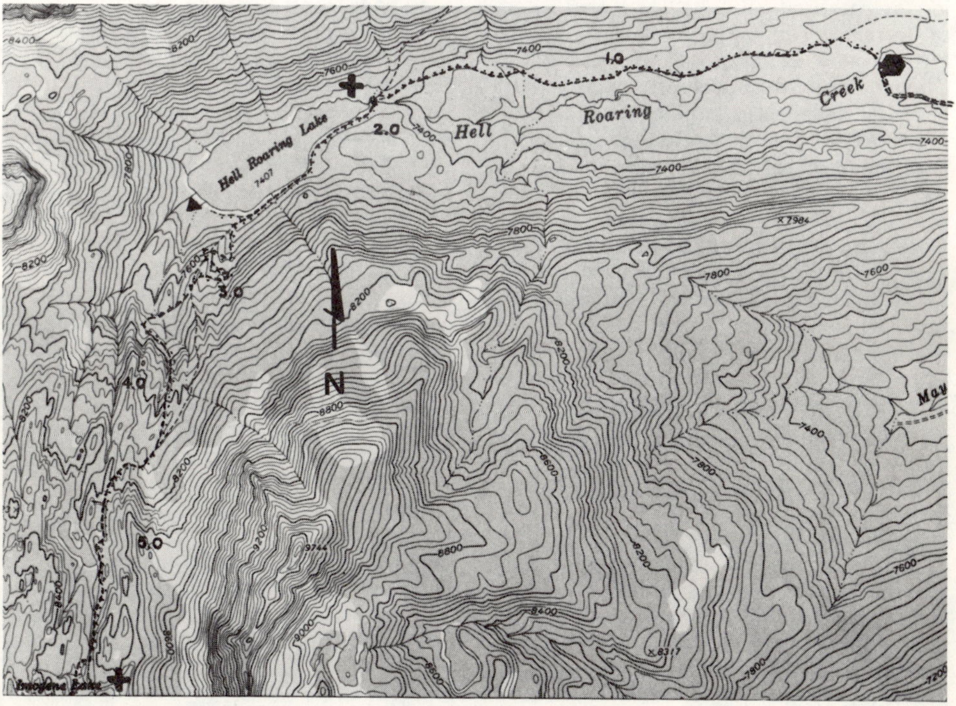

34 CRAMER LAKES

Distance: 7.7 miles
Elevation gain: 1,780 feet
High point: 8,380 feet
Allow 5 hours
Open July to November
Topographic map:
  U.S.G.S. Mt. Cramer
    7.5′ 1963
  U.S.G.S. Warbonnet Peak
    7.5′ 1972

This hike seems almost European, what with the boat ride across big Redfish Lake to the trailhead and then the narrow, verdant valley with high peaks shouldered by snowfields so reminiscent of the Alps. But the thick forest in the valley and the trout in the eleven lakes accessible from the trail remind one it's the old non-pareil, The American West. This trail climbs steadily for almost 8 miles, playing tag with Redfish Lake Creek that is fed by torrents dropping from lateral cirques high up on either valley wall. It ends at the 3 Cramer Lakes, the upper two exceptionally beautiful and hence, popular. A side trail climbs to Alpine Lake, offering spectacular panoramas of the valley below, and then switchbacks down to Baron Lakes. From here it's an easy hike to Stevens Lakes. Farther up the main trail you can find solitude and excellent brook trout fishing by brush-whacking up rivulets to the Upper Redfish Lakes.

From Stanley drive 5 miles south on U.S. 93 to the Redfish Lake Visitors Center sign and turn right and drive 2 miles to the lodge. Inside at the registration desk make arrangements for a boat ride across the lake ($6 round-trip in '77) to the transfer camp. Before leaving double check with the attendant about date and hour for your rendezvous and return trip and write it down.

Shoulder your pack and follow a trace left up to the fenced transfer camp. Walk west to the outhouse in the center, turn 40 degrees right and in 90 yards reach a sign just outside the fence stating Bench Lakes and Lily Pond. Behind this sign is a box and sign marking the Redfish Lake Cr. Trail to Cramer Lakes. Register at the box and begin climbing moderately in forest for .3 miles, catching glimpses of the creek's cascades on your left, then switchback twice right across an open hillside, where a jagged spine forms the left valley wall and diminishes into the valley's head. Gray cliffs blotched with brown rear on your right. At .6 mile keep left at a fork, cross a rockslide and ease into a short descent, only to climb steeply to begin a moderate irregular traverse at 1 mile. Across the creek 150 yards cliffs rise in both spires and angular knobs, as if the sculptor couldn't decide. Ahead .2 mile cross a clearing, then another, and suddenly descend into tall, cool timber, crossing waterboards and then 2 rivulets to reach the creek at 2.4 miles. Switchback steeply right, then descend to Slide Rock Pool, a chute of foaming white water polishing exposed granite, and continue descending to a rockslide at 3.0 miles. Now climb erratically through woods to a bridge at 3.4 miles where the left wall is actually 2 separate peaks punctuated by crevices spewing fans of alluvium. Ahead the valley widens to reveal snow-blotched peaks that shade Upper Redfish Lakes.

Wind through jackpines to a fork at 4.1 miles, ignoring the right to Alpine and Baron Lakes. To reach Upper Redfish Lakes begin your cross-country hike here. Take the left fork now, across Redfish Lake Creek and climb gently through timber across 4 sets of water boards, and at 5.0 miles veer left and begin climbing moderately to steeply, switchbacking long and steeply at 5.6 miles where there's a great view of the peaks and snowfields. Climb another .6 miles and ease to gentle undulation through a pass and into a twisting corridor through lodgepoles that leads to Lower Cramer Lake at 7.7 miles. Jagged peaks rise so close on all sides it seems improbable this basin holds 3 lakes. The trail leads on to the upper lakes, of which the middle is the most striking.

Camping is abundant on all shores of the lower lake, along the west shore of the middle, and the north of the upper. All the lakes are overpopulated with brookies that seldom exceed 8 inches, and they are readily caught on flies in the shallows. For photographs of goats hike to the peaks above Upper Redfish Lakes.

Lower Cramer Lake

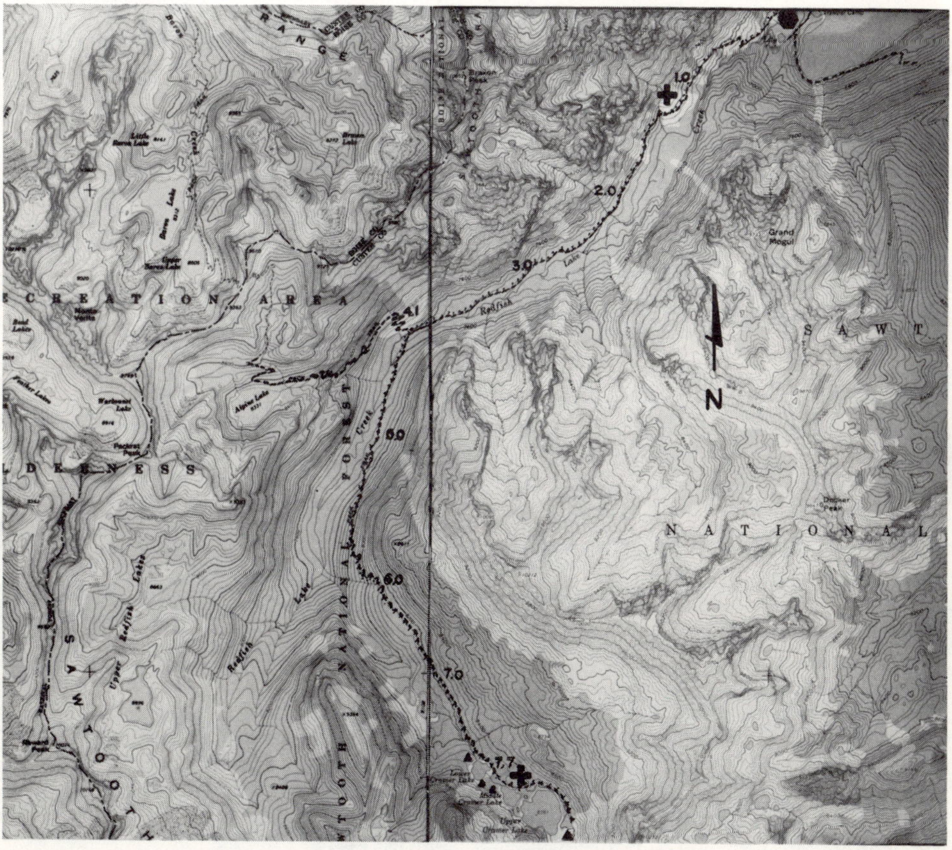

35 BENCH LAKES

Distance: 4 miles
Elevation gain: 1,175 feet
High point: 7,740 feet
Allow 2.5 hours
Open late June through October
Topographic map:
  U.S.G.S. Mt. Cramer
  7.5′ 1963
  U.S.G.S. Stanley
  7.5′ 1963

The trail to Bench Lakes climbs along a lateral moraine shouldering Redfish Lake's glacier-scooped bed, affording magnificent views of it, and ends at a cluster of lakes below jagged Mount Heyburn—a good place for a walk-up ascent. Continuing up Redfish Lake Creek will take one to Cramer Lakes. Begin this hike at dawn because it starts in open sage and the last third is under the sun's glare.

Drive about 5 miles south of Stanley on U.S. 93 and turn right at the Redfish Lake Visitor's Center sign and drive 1 mile to a sign on the right stating Backpacker Parking Area and park in the grassy clearing.

From the parking lot's west end walk on a road about 400 feet to a sign and turn right onto a trail and traverse moderately .2 mile, then left for 120 yards to a fork in open sage. Bear left 75 yards to another fork and keep left, climbing along the north side of the ridge, crossing to the south side at .8 mile with the lake showing through the trees. Soon veer right into a dry wash, then round a bend and suddenly see jagged peaks through the trees. Climb for 2 miles winding moderately along the ridge under tall trees that change at 2.8 miles to chaparral and stunted pines. A forested ridge across a swale on the right sweeps up to Mount Heyburn's 8 minarets in a crown. Redfish is a long, blue fiord 900 feet below billowed with sails of weekend norsemen's fiberglass craft. At 3.1 miles bear right at a fork, then left going up Redfish Creek to Cramer Lakes, and dip into the swale to a registration box, then switchback moderately for .4 mile and veer left to a brook. Climb beside it to the first lake at 4.0 miles. Continue on the level 200 yards to a second lake.

There are level campsites between the first and second lakes, and near the outlets of the two above. All of them hold brook trout, although friends claim they've caught cutthroats. The trout average 7 inches, and a dozen years of heavy fishing pressure hasn't decimated the naturally reproducing population that takes small dark flies fished from shore. During evening and morning midge hatches No. 22's are mandatory.

*Angler and brook trout
at Lower Bench Lake*

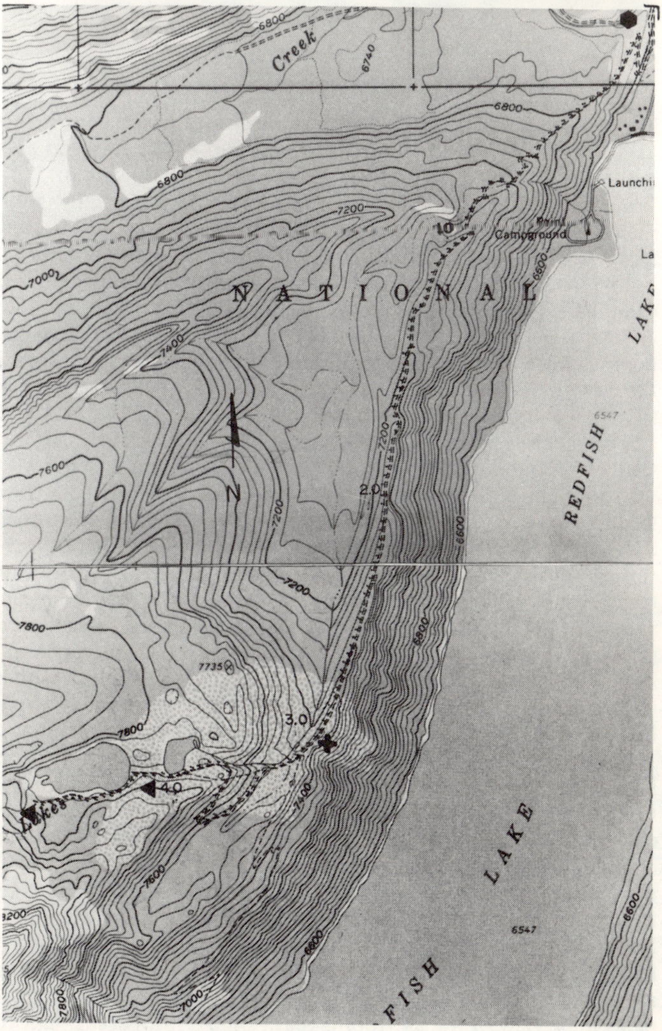

36 MARSHALL LAKE

Distance: 5 miles
Elevation gain: 1,600 feet; loss: 300 feet
High point: 8,200 feet
Allow 3 hours
Open mid-June through October
Topographic map:
U.S.G.S. Stanley
7.5' 1963

Marshall Lake is a clear, cold gem on the lower flanks of the Sawtooth's front slope. Although it is near the popular Alpine Way Trail, most hikers stop only for a gander on their way to Goat or Sawtooth Lake, then move on, so that in addition to excellent brook trout fishing it provides uncrowded camping. The trail is shaded most of the way and never very steep, and pauses above Fishhook Creek's canyon for a stunning view of the Sawtooths that makes this a must route for area photographers. Two isolated lakes can be reached by the ambitious from Marshall by scrambling.

From Stanley drive 3 miles south on U.S. 93 and a quarter-mile past the Stanley SNRA sign watch for a road and sign on the right stating Alpine Way Trail where the highway turns abruptly left, and turn right. Drive 400 yards to another Alpine Way Trail sign and turn left and dip down a hill to yet another sign. You can park here or follow the track right from the sign another .7 mile and park in lodgepole woods.

Climb gently through pines and grassy understory for .3 mile then switchback twice to join the Alpine Way Trail at .8 mile. Quickly reach a 3-way fork and keep right, climbing moderately through ground huckleberries to a ridgetop at 1.3 miles. Continue through aspens across a small clearing, then into woods in 4 switchbacks to a registration box on a sagebrush knoll at 1.5 miles. Climb along the ridge .2 miles and veer left for a panoramic view of the Sawtooths that would take your breath away if you weren't out of it. Descend gently through open woods and flowers for 1.1 miles then at 2.9 miles climb erratically and often steeply over 3 ridges then swing right into a level traverse at 3.9 miles. After .5 mile of beautiful tilted meadow enter trees and veer right to a crest and see Marshall Lake glimmering through the trees on the left below towering rock cliffs split by a waterfall you can hear.

Descend in 4 moderate switchbacks to a fork at 4.9 and keep right another .1 mile and turn left along the lake's north shore and walk to the west end for a flat camping site. From here 2 waterfalls are visible coming down from the lake a thousand feet higher. Another lake 3 times Marshall's size can be reached by switchbacking back up the ridge, across the meadow traverse, and then hiking due west. Marshall's trout reproduce, so take your limit to help keep the population balanced with the food supply. The tree-lined marshy shores dictate waders for fly-fishermen. By late August the brookies will be lying on the bottom, awaiting the evening flight of winged reddish ants or a spinnerfall of *Callibaetis americanus*. In late September most Sawtooth lakes from 7 to 8,000 feet have hatches of winged black ants and hatches of *Paraleptophlebia packii*, with heavy evening rises of hundreds of trout the rule while morning and afternoon fishing is slow. However, fishing midge pupal flies on a slow-sinking line along the bottom will net an occasional afternoon trout.

Sawtooth Range from Marshall Lake Trail

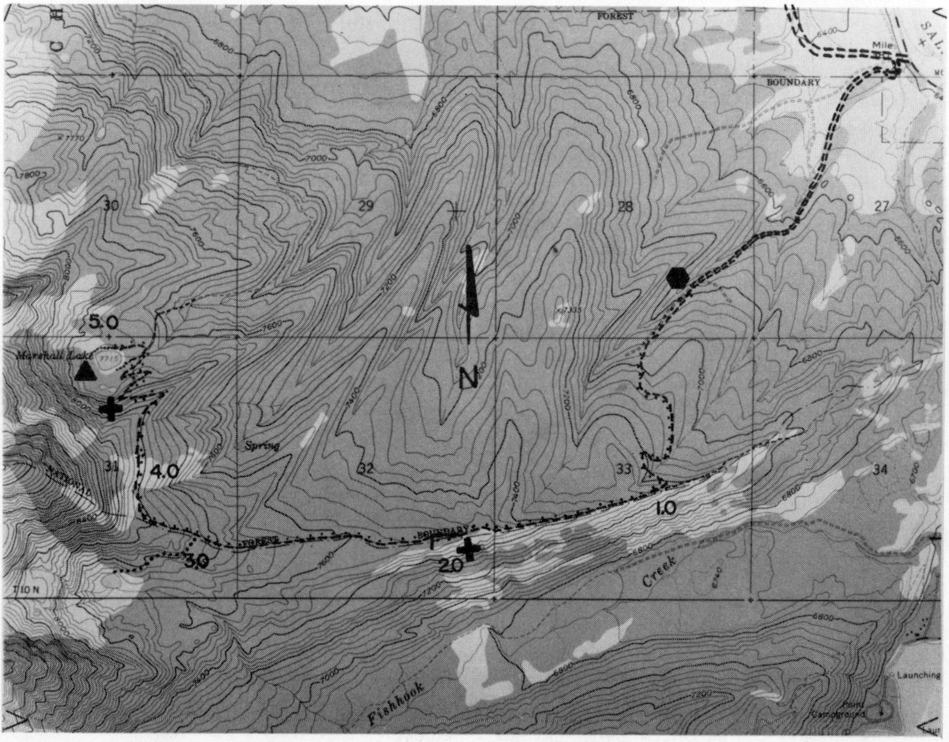

37 SAWTOOTH LAKE

Distance: 5.2 miles
Elevation gain: 1,740 feet
High point: 8,450 feet
Allow 3.5 hours
Open July to November
Topographic map:
  U.S.G.S. Stanley Lake
  7.5′ 1972

It's impossible to have a favorite hike in the Sawtooths because they're all unique in their own ways and all spectacular. But Iron Creek Trail to Sawtooth Lake boasts a little of everything: a trail through quiet forest beside a clear stream, a canyon with cliffs and peaks close enough to bounce echoes off, big lakes and little, meadows, trout fishing for 2 species, and access to cross-country routes. Sawtooth Lake itself is large as alpine lakes go. It seems to miraculously perch on the final, highest spire of the Sawtooth Range's backbone, with the upper fourth of Mount Regan rising from the lake's depths at one end. For an extended stay one can strike out from a base at Sawtooth and reach McGowan, Regan, and Trail Lakes after short cross-country hikes.

Drive 2 miles west from Stanley on Idaho 21 and turn left at the Iron Creek Road sign, drive 4 miles to a fork, keeping right for .2 mile to another fork and sign where you go right into Iron Creek Transfer Camp. The trail begins at a large signboard depicting various Sawtooth trails.

Wind on the level through lodgepoles and grass and flowers with solid forest on the right and on your left a mountain so sheer it seems impossible those scattered trees don't lose their grip. Pass a marshy meadow and meet the creek at .5 mile, then veer right and left up a hillock to a wilderness boundary at 1.1 miles. Ahead a rock wall rises over 2,400 feet, giving one the sense of being lorded over. Past the sign reach a meadow on the left; from it downstream the creek holds Dolly Varden and cutthroat trout that bear much pressure, so please release all trout caught. Turn right and climb gently another .8 mile then up a steep pitch to a sign directing you left. Traverse gently for .3 mile, make 3 moderate switchbacks, then another gentle traverse with moderate stretches crossing the basin at Iron Creek's head at 3.3 miles. On its far side look back at the serrated ridge, a paragon of all Sawtooth skylines. Make 14 moderate switchbacks to another fork at 4.1 miles. Left 400 feet is deep green Alpine Lake, itself worth the hike. Golden trout feed at its west end.
Take the right fork and climb in 16 moderate switchbacks, cross a rivulet at 4.7 miles and curve left and descend gently past a tarn on the right, over a brook and up a hill to a fork at 5.2 miles. The lake is through the trees a few feet left.

Either camp by the tarn or continue left around the lake to the far end. Trout feed out from shore, so to consistently catch the small brookies fly casters will need a float tube. Keep all fish caught, as the lake is overpopulated. To reach McGowan, Regan, and Trail Lakes take the right fork around the lake's north end. These lakes can be easily fished from shore. Release all golden trout in Alpine Lake, as there's no reproduction, and the population is dwindling, since the Fish and Game Dept. currently has no source of eggs or fry to restock it.

Afternoon angler at Alpine Lake

Sawtooth Lake

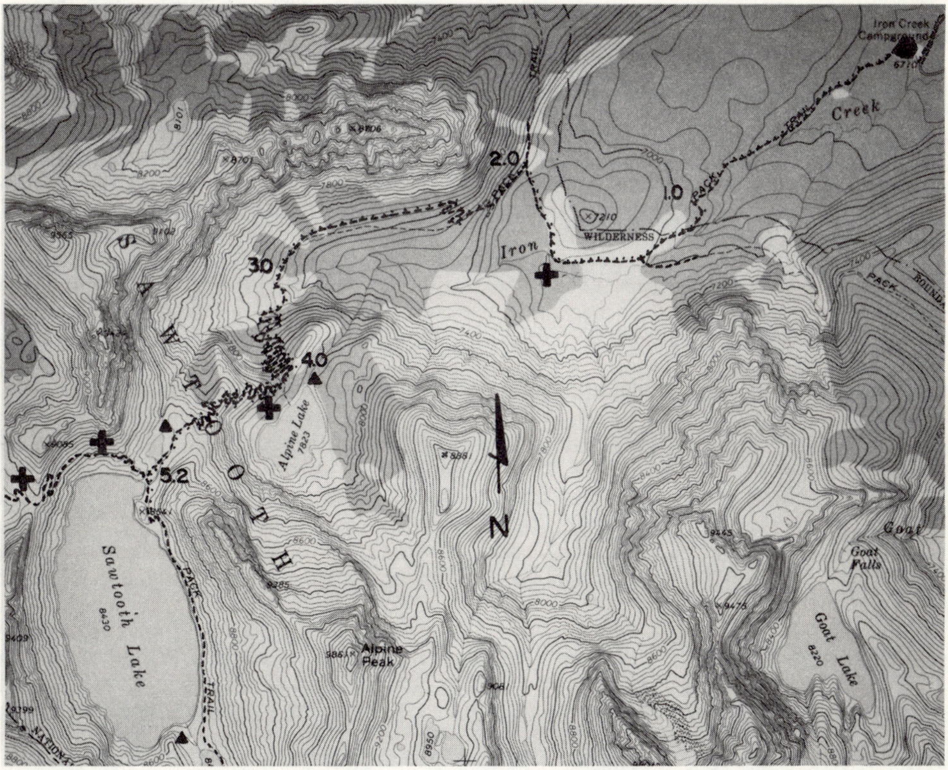

38 HANSON LAKES

Distance: 4.7 miles
Elevation gain: 1,350 feet
High point: 7,941 feet
Allow 3 hours
Open July through October
Topographic map:
  U.S.G.S. Stanley Lake
  7.5′ 1972

The hike to Hanson Lakes offers a multitude of options. The gentle lower trail—really a road reverting back to trail—passes meadows and 2 nice waterfalls with McGown's spectacular face visible all the way; one needn't scramble up the near-vertical ascent the last half-mile to Hanson Lakes to have outstanding scenery. A weekend trip is possible without climbing to Hanson by continuing past the fork up Stanley Creek another 3 miles where spur trails lead to McGown Lakes (cutthroats), Trail Creek Lakes (large rainbows), and Regan Lake (golden trout). If you've children too small for the steep, follow the main trail to the summit from where you can look down Trail Creek's canyon. There are beautiful campsites beside the creek all the way.

But if you should opt for the very steep climb past Bridal Veil Falls to Hanson Lakes, you'll find 3 beautiful lakes in high basin-country frequented by mule deer bucks and goats. There's lots of crest area to explore up here.

From Stanley drive about 6 miles west on Idaho 21 to a sign and fork stating Stanley Lake 3 Miles left. Drive 3 miles to a fork and sign stating Stanley Lake Campground left Inlet C.G. straight and go right .5 mile to a sign stating Inlet C.G. A&B and bear right at a Pay Fee sign to the road's end and park under trees. The trail begins at the fence and sign announcing the Alpine Way Trail 7 Miles.

Cross the fence and walk the road, winding through 8-foot-high willows and meadows graced on the left by Stanley Creek's placid flowage reflecting McGown Peak's ragged 3,400-foot face, and at .5 mile

reach a sign blurting "Trail." From this point upstream to Lady Face Falls Stanley Creek has fair Dolly Varden and Eastern Brook Trout fishing. Bear right from the sign and meadow-meander .7 mile to a sign stating Iron Creek 6 Miles and in 130 yards register at a box. Cross a rivulet and .8 mile of meadow and lodgepole pine and enter woods. Climb moderately to a spring at 2.0 miles. Thick forest obscures any view to the right.

Dogleg left across a rockslide, then veer right on a double track to a hill at 2.5 and a tiny sign on the right announcing Lady Face falls down in the woods on the left. Descend moderately to Stanley Creek, cross to its left bank, and climb moderately for .7 mile to a sign at 3.8 directing you right to Bridal Veil Falls. Follow a trail 180 yards crossing the creek and wind uphill through willows for 70 yards where the trail splits. Angle right towards the hill across an old slash heap to Hanson Creek at 4.0 miles.

The falls isn't visible from here, although several scramble trails attempt to reach a viewpoint. For a view of the falls, walk 150 yards right from the creek to a very clear but sheer path up a gulley, and climb it for .1 mile until the ridge on your left becomes a rocky spine offering hand and foot holds, then shift left to its more secure footing. From here the falls, really a steep long cascade, is visible. To reach Hanson Lakes continue up the spine, which the gulley path soon joins, and after .5 mile reach a sloping rock ridge culminating in several pinnacles. On your left far up the creek you can see 9,850-foot Rhino Horn Peak.

Follow a legible path at a steep grade along the ridge-crest which soon broadens into a forested slope, which gradually angles left to join the creek's rushing sound at 4.7 miles. Through the trees you'll see Lower Hanson Lake. Best camping is along the northeast and southeast shores. Trout cruise at the south and west ends. To reach the upper lakes angle 45 degrees uphill from the outlet creek for 200 feet. While cutthroats to 16″ are plentiful below, they're scarce and larger in the middle lake, found mostly near its west and north shores, and should be released. There's camping space for two tents along the southeast ridge, but hardly any at the third, upper lake, which has no fish.

Sawtooth Skyline from Lower Hanson Lake

Lower Hanson Lake by moonlight

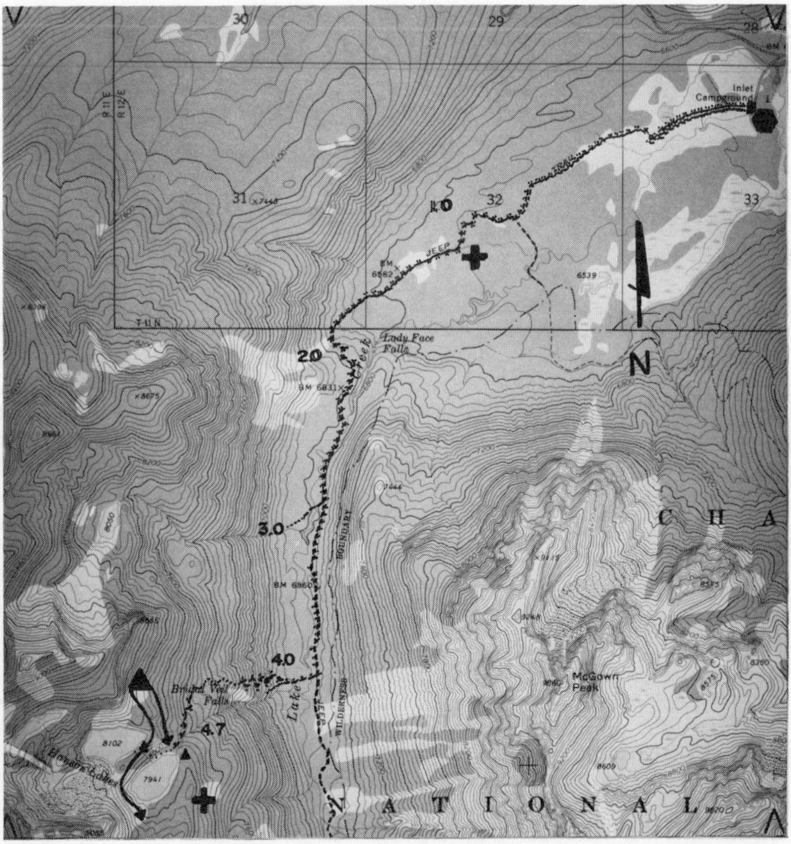

39 RUFFNECK PEAK

Distance: 4.8 miles
Elevation gain: 2,300 feet
High point: 9,407 feet
Allow 3.5 hours
Open mid-June through October
Topographic map:
U.S.G.S. Capehorn Lakes
7.5′ 1972
U.S.G.S. Langer Peak
7.5′ 1972

Ruffneck Peak, selected by the forest service as a lookout site because it commands a wide expanse of mountains, offers to hikers a grand view south over Stanley Basin to the Sawtooth and White Cloud Ranges and west of the vast blue-timbered ridges of the Idaho Primitive Area. The Maishu Trail leads into rolling forest and small but precipitous crags with lush meadows and alpine lakes at their bases. Off the main trail one can take easy cross-country routes to secluded lakes containing rainbow, cutthroat, and brook trout and offering empty campsites. By taking the Halstead Cr. trail down Ruffneck Ridge towards Beaver Cr. Campground you can reach 8 other large lakes flanking the trail which traverses wilderness country. Deer and elk summer here, but goats are scarce.

This wild roadless area is being considered for inclusion in the Idaho Wilderness Area, and to insure its inclusion letters to Cecil Andrus, Secretary of the Interior, are encouraged. A small-time miner has already bulldozed the Seafoam Lake trail into a jeep trail with Forest Service approval.

From Stanley drive about 19 miles west on Idaho 21 and where it veers 90 degrees left turn right onto a dirt road at a sign stating Lolo Creek Campground-Seafoam Area and in 40 yards bear right at a fork and sign stating Seafoam Area. Drive about 8.5 miles, passing a Bradley Memorial Boy Scout Camp sign you ignore on the right and at another fork and sign stating Ruffneck Peak 8 Miles left keep right on the main road to a sharp right turn and sign on the right stating Beaver Creek-Greyhound Tr. Ruffneck L.O. 6 miles. Park in one of several narrow pullouts near this sign.

Across the road from the sign is a stone monument. Walk 30 feet right from it to the trail which leads 90 feet uphill to a Maishu Trail sign, from which you climb left through open woods and pine-needle floor, crossing a rivulet at .1 mile. At .6 begin a rubble path and in .3 mile reach a ridgetop. Ahead blue sky shows through trees. On your right a steep white granite-and-conifer hillside rises, and 2 miles away on the left across a forested basin a ridge of low cliffs curves right to merge with Ruffneck Peak, occasionally visible ahead.

Climb gently to moderately in woods across a rock-strewn understory, up a steep incline at 1.5, then another and traverse across a shallow coulee that fans out into a lodgepole and fir flat. Across the flat climb over a low ridge to Bear Creek at 2.3 miles. Cross another rivulet and top a knoll from which you can see Ruffneck Peak rearing 1400 feet 2 miles away. Descend moderately 80 yards and spot Langer Lake at 2.5 miles through the trees on the right. Its shore is tree-lined and crowded by berry bushes. Best campsites are along the southeast and north shores. Its rainbow trout to 11″ congregate at the west end. Rocky Lake, an easy 30-minute hike north of Langer, offers even better fishing.

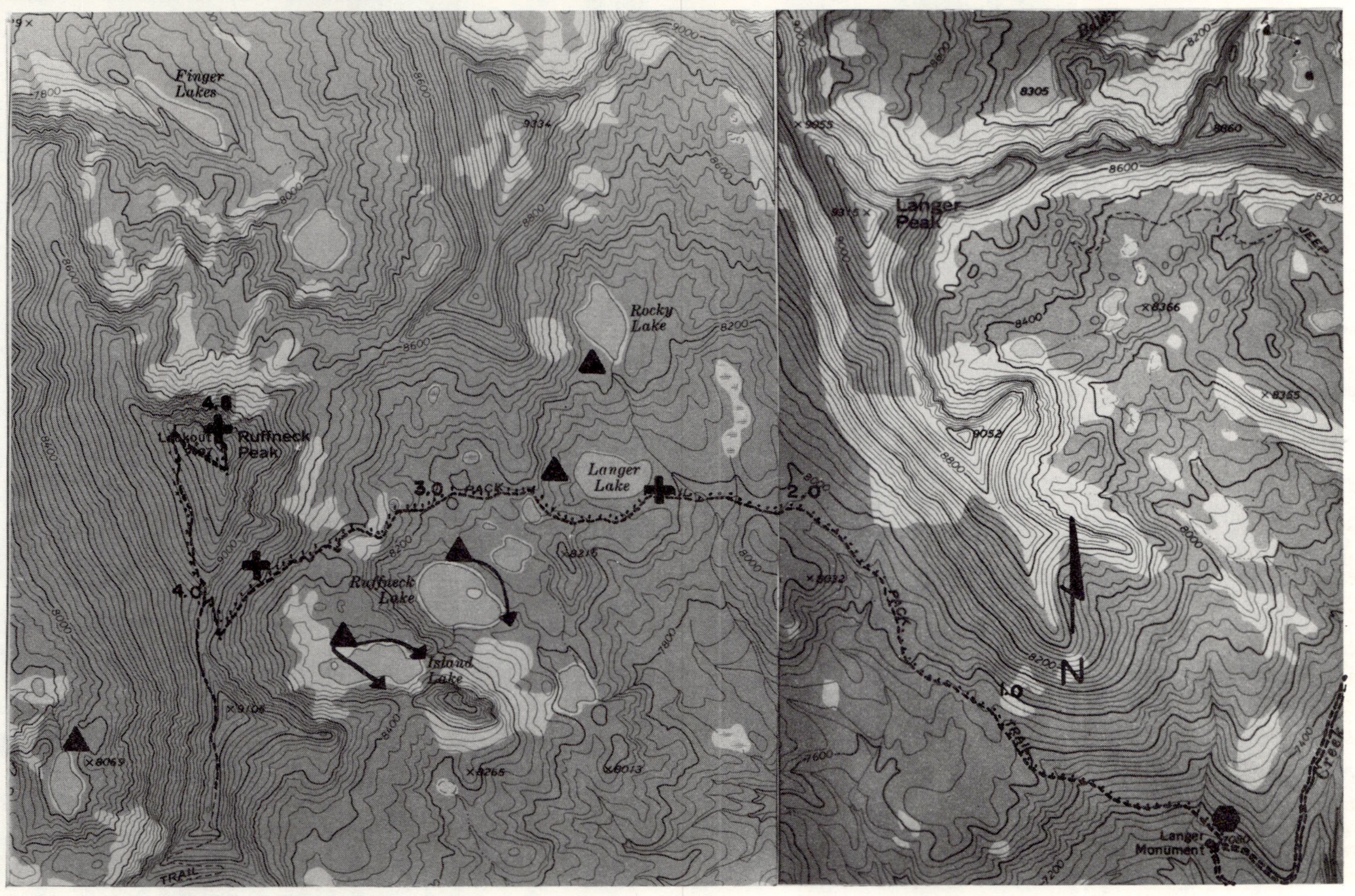

Finger Lakes
Rocky Lake
Langer Lake
Lookout (Ruffneck Peak)
Ruffneck Lake
Island Lake
Langer Peak
Langer Monument
JEEP
PACK TRAIL
PACK TRAIL
TRAIL
N
2.0
3.0 PACK
4.0
1.0

Brook trout from F87 Lake near Ruffneck Peak

But on to Ruffneck Peak. From the Maishu sign climb erratically but never steeply for .2 mile through grassy, open woods to a sign stating Ruffneck L.O. 2 miles. Climb another .2 mile to a flat, dry meadow and traverse moderately to a pond where you veer left from Ruffneck's rocky shoulder, then turn 90 degrees right to a viewpoint at 3.2 miles. Below 5 lakes glint, and the Sawtooth and White Cloud Ranges jag the horizon. Skirt a small basin, cross a hillock, and begin traversing steeply with very steep pitches above another basin and lake through scrub firs, with Ruffneck leaning over you on the right. At 3.8 switchback right and left to a sign at 4.0 stating Ruffneck L.O. right. By hiking left you'd reach the basins of Fall Creek Lake No. 1 (brook trout) and No. 2 (cutthroats), and Mable Lakes (small brookies).

Traverse steeply right for .5 mile in scrub timber, endless timbered ridges of the Primitive Area rippling away to the western horizon, their rubble-rock summits spilling angular patches of rockslides down their slopes. Turn right for 350 yards, then left to reach the L.O. at 4.8 miles. Walk to its north side and look down on the long, green Finger Lakes and another round one. All contain rainbow trout.

Climb steeply .2 mile to a sign at a fork stating the Maishu Trail right. To reach Island and Ruffneck Lakes go left down a faint trail to a pond and from its far side drop downhill to Ruffneck, a deep, rock-bound home for rainbow and cutthroat trout to 17''. From its island go left 400 yards and you can follow an outlet .3 mile to another small lake with excellent rainbow fishing and limited natural reproduction, or continue around Ruffneck to another creek that leads to Island Lake where the best fishing is along its northwest end. There is limited camping space along Ruffneck's shore and many sites at Island Lake.

Ruffneck Peak and Langer Lake

40 HORSESHOE LAKE

Distance: 4.6 miles
Elevation gain: 1,400 feet; loss: 685 feet
High point: 8,680 feet
Allow 3 hours
Open late June to November
Topographic map:
  U.S.G.S. Knapp Lakes
  7.5′   1964

This is a true wilderness trace, receiving a fraction of the traffic borne by any Sawtooth trail. The trail winds through forest and shade all the way, with wildflowers brightening the mostly grass forest floor. One could hike for a week here among nearly 20 lakes and never retrace one's footsteps. The peaks rising from these lakes top 9,000 feet, with Tango Peak above Horseshoe Lake the highest at 10,000. Scenery is nearly equal to the Sawtooths, the fishing better, and the opportunity for solitude is infinitely greater. Elk summer in the valley and some goats roam the crags. The adventurous can strike out for miles north, east, or south and never leave alpine lake country.

Drive 19 miles west from Stanley on Idaho 21 and turn right at the sign stating Capehorn Guard Station right. Follow the road 5.5 miles, passing the Jones Ranch sign and the Guard Station's sign, and turn right at the Knapp Creek Road sign. Drive on graded gravel for 3 miles, then you'd better have a high-clearance auto for the next 3 miles, which brings you to a mudhole. If you can cross it you'll reach a sign at 2.6 miles from the hole stating Knapp Lakes 4 miles left, Hindman Lake 5 miles right.

Take the left fork and wind through a level meadow, the road's double track soon narrowing to trail in lush woods. Catch glimpses above the trees of rocky peaks on the right whose snowfields feed the lakes at their bases, and at .7 mile cross a creek, then a low ridge to another meadow from which you cut 90 degrees right, across Knapp Creek. The old trail goes left here. Veer left and climb gently beneath tall firs in an understory of huckleberries, grass, and flowers for 0.6 mile, surmount a low ridge and cross Knapp Creek to intersect the old trail at 1.9 miles. Climb gently another mile then up a steep pitch away from the creek, dip across a brook, and continue moderately across open timber with the high peaks above Knapp Lakes 2 airmiles away on the right. Enter an old burn at 2.9 miles, from which you can leave the trail and hike on fairly level ground by contouring to Knapp Lakes and their lovely campsites and naturally reproducing cutthroats to 16 inches. From the burn wind steeply uphill through thinning timber to a saddle and an old Forest Service sign at 3.9 miles pointing over the divide to Loon Creek's long forested valley and Horseshoe Lake below you at Loon's head, a crystalline emerald color with dark spruces on the inside of the horseshoe. Traverse downhill steeply, winding for .7 mile through woods to the lake.

Campsites are along all shores except the western. Cutthroat trout to 14 inches are abundant in this deep lake. The creek 2 miles below holds cutthroats and small Dolly Vardens.

Horseshoe Lake

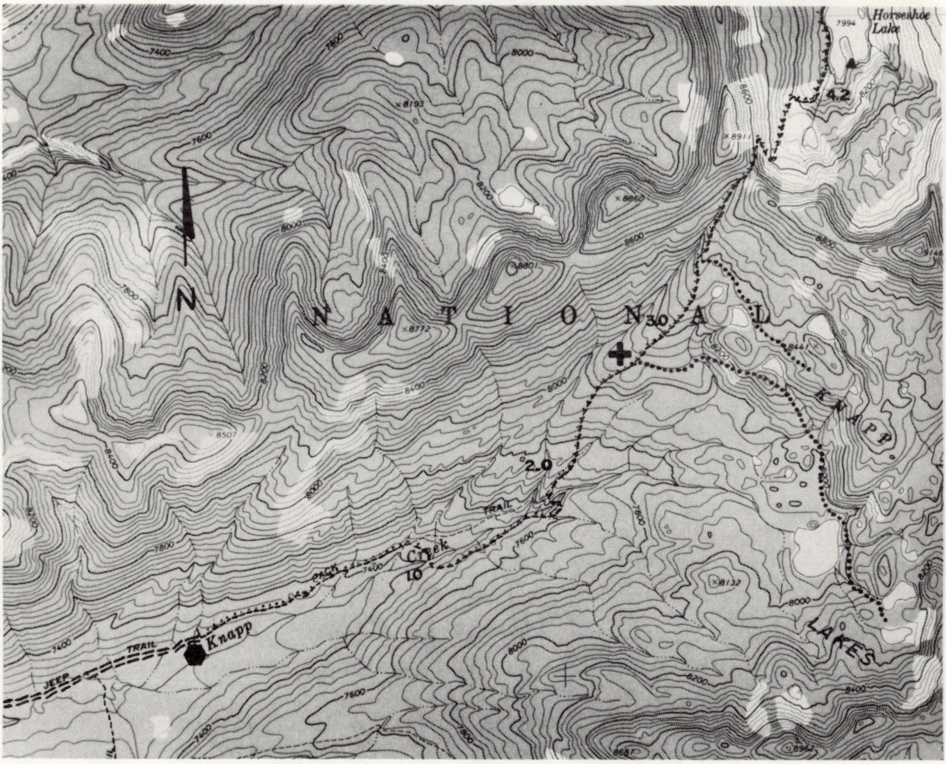

41 SOLDIER LAKES

Distance: 4 miles
Elevation gain: 480 feet; loss: 620 feet
High point: 8,040 feet
Allow 2.5 hours
Open July to November
Topographic map:
  U.S.G.S. Greyhound Ridge
  15′   1961

This lake group nestles below short, precipitous peaks sprouting along the top of low forested hills forming the top of a mountain range whose foot is 5,000 feet below at the bank of the Middle Fork of the Salmon River. Hopefully, with the urging of letter-writers enamoured with the area, it will become part of the proposed River of No Return Wilderness, a possibility now in the hands of Secretary of the Interior Cecil Andrus. Some 24 lakes nestle in cirques worn in granite, this being the eastern edge of the Idaho Batholith, the world's largest granite upheaval, and almost all contain reproducing populations of native cutthroat trout. Though the area is relatively small, one seldom knows what's over the next ridge because it's composed of a jumble of close, heavily-forested ridges that eliminate sweeping vistas. Goats, elk, deer, bear and cougar are abundant, though chances of seeing one of the elusive cats is nil. This is an excellent family wilderness camping area, with no developed sites, a change of scenery possible every day without a long hike on gentle trails. A panoramic view of the Middle Fork's canyon and the largest *de facto*

wilderness in the contiguous U.S. is possible by hiking from Soldier Lakes via Cutthroat Lakes to Big Soldier Mountain.

Follow directions in trail No. 39 to the Beaver Creek-Greyhound Tr. Ruffneck L.O. sign, but instead of parking continue on the main road over Vanity summit another 8 miles to a fork and sign stating Josephus Lake left. Don't attempt to travel this road at night, for the strictly one-land stretches edging an 800-foot cliff offer no turnaround and a dangerous option of backing up should one meet another vehicle. *Do not* attempt to pull a camper trailer over Vanity pass and on to Josephus Lake. Turn left and at a fork in 2.5 miles ignore a left turn to Seafoam mine and bear right to Josephus Lake in another 2 miles.

Park by the bridge across Josephus Creek and walk right along the shore up a hillock to a registration box, where the trail suddenly begins. Traverse around the lake's right side in steep pitches linked by gentle ones. Across the small valley forest barely fails to reach the top of broken angular granite crags. At 1.5 miles leave sight of the lake and dip into a cool glen and brook called "Mushroom Springs," then cross a meadow into a gulley at 1.7, and climb moderately to a fork. The left goes to Ruffneck Peak but you continue right up a steep ridge and down to Helldiver Lake at 2.1 miles. It is forested all around its shoreline with a low pyramidal peak at its far end.

Climb steeply away from Helldiver for .8 mile in a series of uphill loops, then traverse to the saddle that separates Josephus Creek from Soldier Creek. Beyond are the timbered ridges of the primitive area. Descend in 7 moderate switchbacks to a pond, skirt its shore on the level, and reach a fork at 3.2 miles and sign directing you left. In .3 mile traverse across a rockslide, several small ridges, and in scrub timber at 3.7 miles pass a sign directing you into a basin below of low but steep forested ridges capped with jagged granite cliffs. Veer right from the sign and descend in 3 switchbacks to First Lieutenant Lake. A half-mile farther is Colonel Lake with better camping in cool forest.

There is unlimited flat ground for camping around Soldier Lakes, and all of them offer excellent fishing from shore. Please release most trout in the first 2 lakes, as they receive considerable pressure.

*Trout breakfast at Outlet Creek of
Cutthroat Lake—Soldier Lakes Trail*

Helldiver Lake from Soldier Lakes Trail

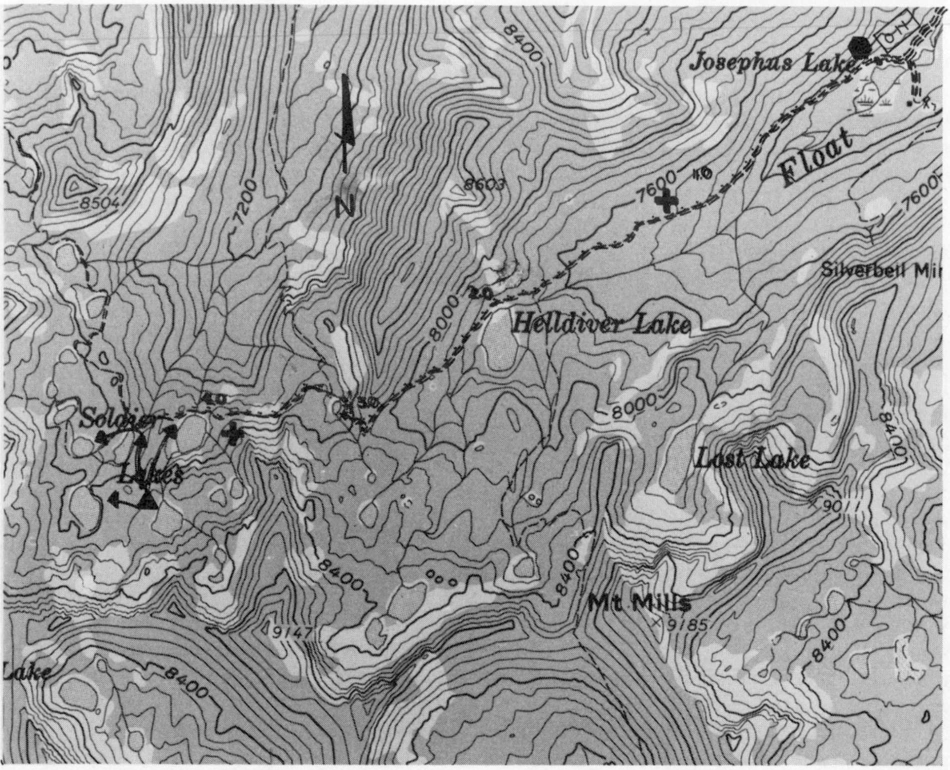

42 WEST FORK LAKES

Distance: 4.4 miles
Elevation gain: 1,560 feet
High point: 8,340 feet
Allow 3 hours
Open late June through October
Topographic map:
  U.S.G.S. Twin Peaks
  15′   1956

The remote trail up West Fork Morgan Creek to the basin and 4 lakes is primitive but well-defined, allowing even the novice hiker to escape crowded trails in the SNRA which are thoroughfares by comparison. Beginning in a narrow timbered canyon beside a rushing trout creek, crossing lawns beneath ponderosa pine, it finally reaches a subalpine basin where many elk summer and goats move stiffly, slowly along the encompassing cliffs. A short hike up the spur trail to White Goat Lookout will give a great panoramic view over the Yellowjacket Mountains as well as a look and access to White Goat Lake and its trout.

Drive 9 miles north on U.S. 93 from Challis and turn left at the Morgan creek Road sign and drive 6 miles to the West Fork Morgan Creek Road and sign and turn left. In 1.5 miles at another fork bear right, heading into West Fork canyon for slightly over 5 miles to the sign, "West Fork Tr. White Goat Lake 7" and turn left onto a side road and park beside a picnic table.

Cross Blowfly Creek at its sign and pass another announcing West Fork Trail. Undulate steeply along the right bank of the creek which flows at a medium gradient between willows and alders on your left. You are against the slope on the right but views up the creek of the canyon's timbered left wall give you a perspective of depth. At 1.2 miles cross the creek and in the shade is a flat grassy lawn perfect for a picnic or game of croquet. A few moments of sneaking along the creek and you'll have 6-inch native trout to supplement your soup—but don't kill more than a brace, for this fragile fishery can't stand much pressure. Continue another mile, then recross the creek and after a long moderate traverse reach a cattle guard at 1.6 miles. High above on the left rise rocky peaks and talus slopes of the high country. Climb gently with occasional steep pitches, the creek always on the left, and at 2.1 miles enter tall trees and grassy, clean forest floor, and reach a creek at 2.6 miles. Climb another .3 to a sign on the right at a fork sending you right 2 miles to West Fork Lakes.

Still on grass under tall ponderosa pine, looping around fallen trees, often a few feet away from a brook, you climb erratically till at 3.7 miles loop right very steeply then left at 4.0 miles across a creek. Loop steeply right, left, cross another brook, and continue in a steep serpentine across a clearing for .3 mile into a traverse through pines along a creek with cliffs close left, and at 4.4 miles see the lake on your left in thick timber.

Camp along the near shore of this shallow pond where California Goldens root in moss for nymphs, or climb up the very steep open slope left of the inlet to the upper lake basin where there's more room. In '77 only the lower lake had trout, with no evidence of reproduction, so please don't come here to kill a limit.

Lower West Fork Trail

Lower West Fork Lake

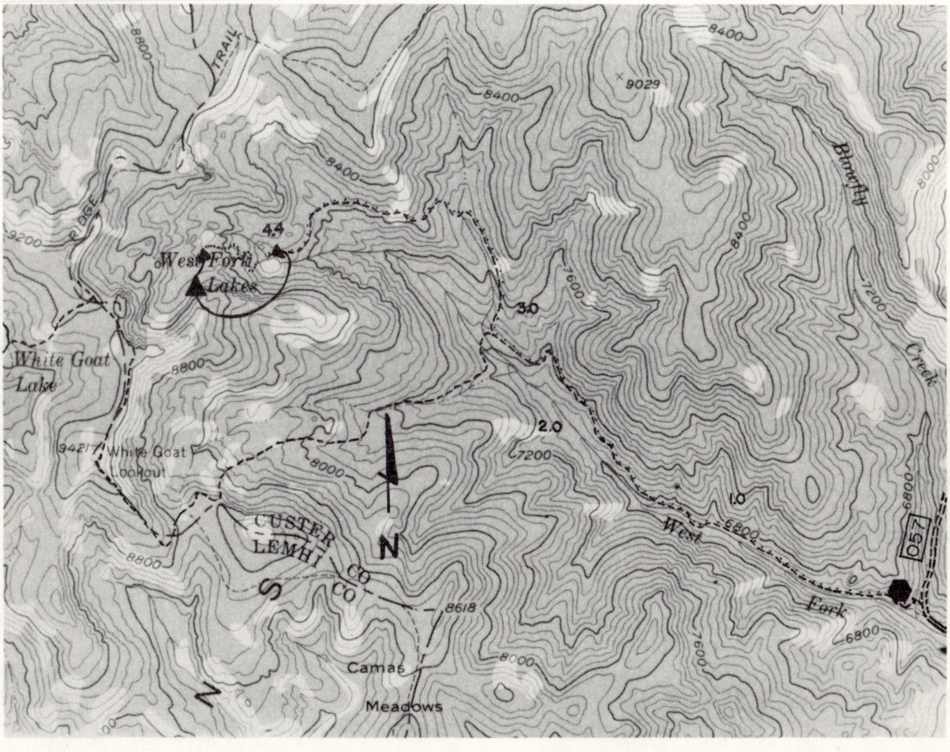

43 GOLDEN TROUT LAKE

Distance: .4 mile
Elevation loss: 300 feet
High point: 8,450 feet
Allow 45 minutes
Open July to late October
Topographic map:
 U.S.G.S. Mount McGuire
 7.5′ 1962

The short hike to this beautiful little lake that belies its name by hosting cutthroat trout provides an excellent steep jaunt for those waiting for hardier or younger cohorts to return from longer treks into the Crags, or for Sunday drivers exploring the backwoods and feeling up to testing their legs. The lake is a lovely picnic or overnight spot, a deep blue gem with an unlittered though oft-visited shoreline that's flat in enough places to accommodate several parties.

Drive to the Bighorn Crags by turning off west from U.S. 93 about 9 miles north of Challis onto Morgan Creek Road. Drive 27 miles to a road fork and sign stating the Bighorn Crags and Cobalt R.S. to the right. Drive 6 miles and turn left at the Porphyry Creek sign also listing the Crags. Porphyry Creek and Panther Creek near the sign are excellent cutthroat and Dolly Varden streams for trout to 2 pounds. Drive another 16 miles to a fork stating Yellowjacket Lake left, Crags Campground right, 11 miles. Don't attempt to haul horses on this road unless your truck is in excellent shape. After 11 steep miles reach the campground and a fork and sign stating Crags C.G. and Transfer C., and keep right for 10 feet to a Corral and Loading Platform sign and again turn right. Drive past the corral on your left,

then veer left around it and on 350 yards to a faint turnaround. Park here and walk 25 yards downhill along a trace of old road, where the trail begins without a sign in a gulley. Be sure to locate this spot, as many people miss the lake by thinking it's so close they don't need the trail.

You're standing on a canyon rim beyond which you can see forested ridges and straight ahead and slightly downhill a jagged spike of granite above Golden Trout, which you can't see for the trees. On your left is the snaggle-toothed rock ridge the Crags Trail follows. Wind downhill on a 2-inch deep trail that exists only in soil between exposed granite that covers most of the hill. At .1 mile veer slightly left for 35 yards over rock, then pick up the trail again as a shallow trough. At this point you should be facing the peak above the lake. Wind steeply for another .1 mile, cross a spring frothy with flowers, then veer left gently for 90 yards to a small bowl from which you'll see the lake through the trees. Descend very steeply without switchbacks for 250 yards and reach the lake at .4 mile.

Camp along the outlet and the eastern shore. Trout here feed sporadically on caddis in early and mid-summer, and on midges later on into October. Some reach 14 inches.

Golden Trout Lake

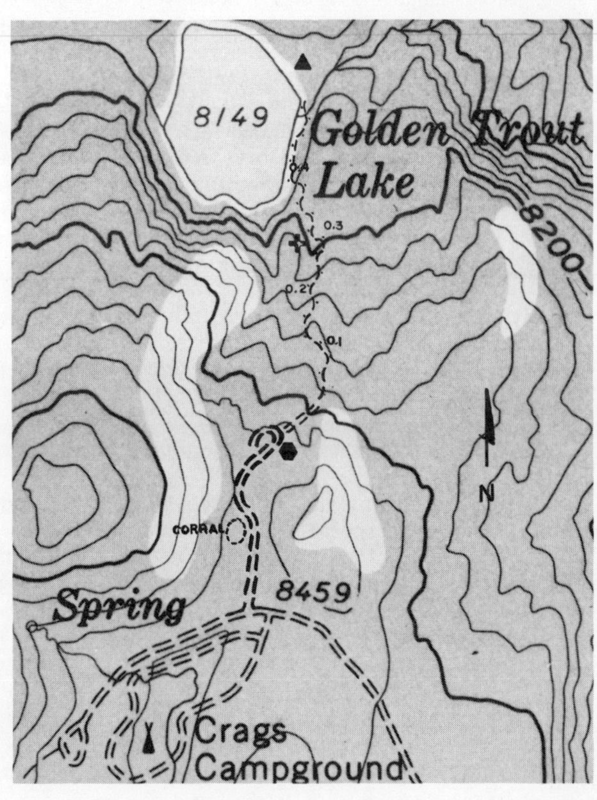

44 CATHEDRAL LAKE

Distance: 4.8 miles
Elevation gain: 500 feet; loss: 690 feet
High point: 8,970 feet
Allow 2.5 hours
Open July to late October
Topographic map:
U.S.G.S. Mount McGuire
7.5′   1962
U.S.G.S. Hoodoo Mdws.
7.5′   1962

This is the first lake one reaches on the Crags Trail, and it breaks you in without killing you, leading past weird knobs of pear-shaped granite 30-100 feet high at a moderate grade, then dropping into a cool, lovely basin and its lake. There is a hint of the granite grandeur of the Crags in 9,411-foot Cathedral Rock above the lake, but just a hint, for those farther along top 10,000 feet with vertical rises exceeding 2,000 feet. An ideal weekend trip without strain is to reach Cathedral late Friday or early Saturday and hike over to Deer Creek Lake, fish and take photos, and hike out Sunday evening. There's no water along the Cathedral Lake trail.

Drive as in trail No. 43 to the Crags Campground, except that at the sign stating Corral and Transfer Camp bear left another 200 feet, then right 20 yards to the turnaround by the pictorial sign depicting the Crags.

Register at the box, then make 3 moderate switchbacks for .2 mile through whitebark and lodgepole pine growing in fragile white granitic soil with exposed slabs of white granite everywhere. Pass above the rim of Golden Trout Lake's basin and veer left to a rise from which you'll see several monoliths like thumbs and pears along the ridge ahead. At .8 mile descend moderately along the ridge through open forest, with several creek-head basins visible over the canyon rim on your right and across the 2,000-foot deep Wilson Creek Canyon on the left the distant line of the Crags' peaks. At 1.9 miles ignore a fork left to Yellowjacket Creek, bearing right to Clear Creek and Welcome Lake. Loop left climbing along the ridge's left slope, blocking your view right but providing a clear view of the Crags. At 2.4 cross back to the ridge's right slope and pass several monoliths, descending moderately towards Cathedral Rock, a huge knob of lichen-blackened granite, and reach a sign at 4.1 miles stating Cathedral Lake and pointing right. Walk 28 paces beyond the sign to a fork and keep right a few feet to 4 blazed conifers marking the trail down to the lake. Wind downhill very steeply .3 mile and level out in a grove of small trees with a park 40 feet away on the right. There are several sawed stumps here. Leave the trail you're on, which goes to Deer Lake, and walk right across a boggy rivulet and park about 90 yards to a rim, beyond which you'll see distant blue hills. Pick up the Cathedral Lake trail here, which runs east along the rim for .1 mile, then turns abruptly right and descends in 5 steep, irregular switchbacks .3 mile to the lake.

The trail goes left around the lake to dry campsites along the shore. Waders or a float tube are necessary to foil trees if you're a fly fisherman, although the chunky cutthroats and rainbows here feed in the shallows and among lily pads at the north end of the lake. There is no natural reproduction so don't kill more than a couple fish.

Cathedral Lake   *Granite Monolith, Cathedral Lake Trail*

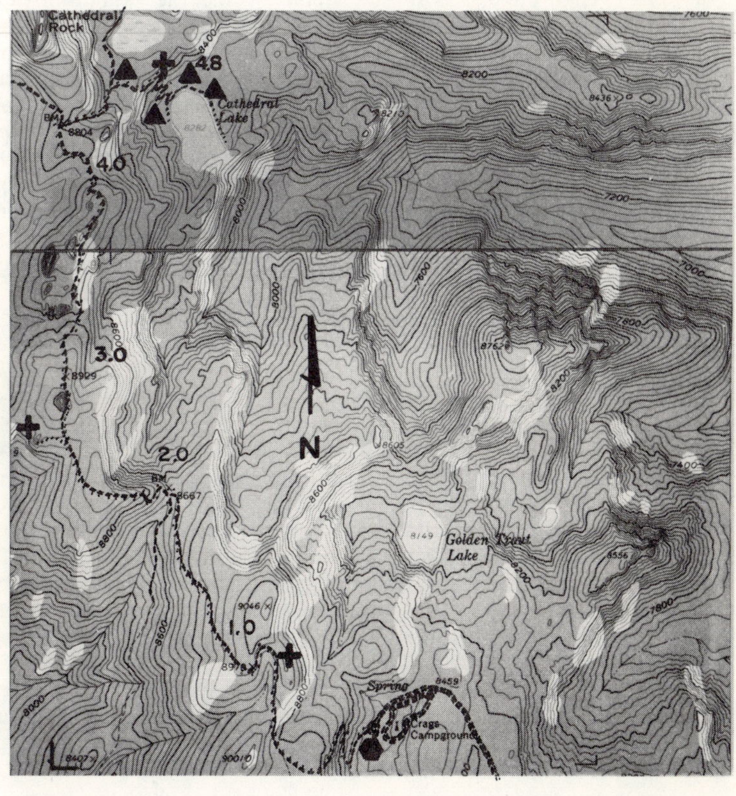

45 DEER LAKE

Distance: 4.2 miles
Elevation gain: 1,400 feet; loss: 1,400 feet
High point: 9,220 feet
Allow 4 hours
Open July to mid-October
Topographic map:
U.S.G.S. Mount McGuire
7.5′ 1962

The main trails of the Bighorn Crags have borne heavy use in recent years, but 3 areas—Deer Creek, Goat Lake, and Wilson Mountain—are seldom visited. Deer Lake and its 2-pound cutthroats lie at the end of a scenic, arduous trail crossing meadows below cliffs and high windswept ridges. A most spectacular, inclusive view of the Crags' 6,000-foot vertical rise is possible from this trail only, as elsewhere peaks block one's view. Yawning timbered canyons branch off from the high ridges making up most of the route.

Follow directions in trail No. 44 to mile 4.2 where you fork right to Cathedral Lake, and instead continue on the trail left. Skirt a meadow's left edge and at .2 mile fill your canteen at a creek issuing from a concave boulder. Veer steeply left from the rivulet watching for small blazes; the trail is seldom used and you'll need to watch carefully for its faint trace. Continue straight uphill through a ragged little meadow, then veer right through whitebark pine forest with a floor of ground huckleberries and white granitic soil and at .6 mile make 5 moderate switchbacks, then traverse to a monolith at 1 mile. Peer around its side for a great view of Cathedral Lake across a forested basin.

Descend along a ridge .2 mile then climb steeply without switchbacks another .2 mile to a benchmark on a tree. Angle left down the ridge for .1 mile on the faintest trail, watching for 4 blazed trees on the left marking the beginning of 13 moderate switchbacks that take you down to a beautiful meadow at 2.1 miles in an amphitheatre with cliff walls looking like granite cubes glued together. Cross the meadow and veer right into a traverse that levels out in a gulch at 2.6 at a tree-imbedded benchmark.

Begin 10 steep switchbacks up a steep sparsely forested hill from which a rare view of the crags is had, and at 3.5 dip into a swale, then steeply up to the ridge and look down 900 feet to Deer Lake. To reach it, walk right along the ridge about 200 yards from where you topped it, and drop down below the cliffs below the crest. Now continue traversing right until you're even with the lake's northern tip, then descend along a sloping avalanche path of scrub timber. If you attempt to reach the lake by dropping down from where you topped the ridge you'll run into cliffs and downed timber, even though the route looks feasible from the top. I know, I tried it first.

The eastern shore has good campsites, as well as the little lake below it. Both the Snake River and Yellowstone varieties of cutthroat trout grow in the lake to 18'', and though they're found all around the lake, its forested shore prohibits fly-fishing without a float tube.

*Breakfast below Cathedral Rock,
beginning of Deer Lake Trail*

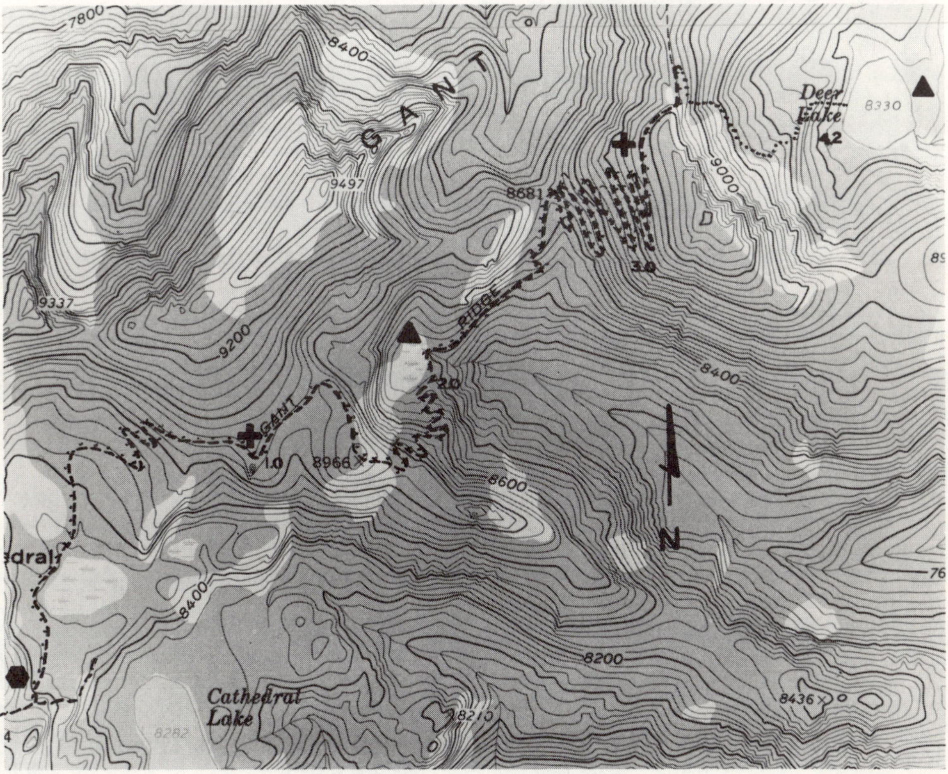

WELCOME LAKE

Distance: 4 miles
Elevation gain: 300 feet; loss: 840 feet
High point: 8,804 feet
Allow 2 hours
Opey July through October
Topographic map:
  U.S.G.S. Mt. McGuire
  7.5′ 1962

Aptly named Welcome Lake is the first lake one meets in the Crags proper via the Waterfall Trail, and if you've hiked the distance between it and Crags Campground in one day, its cool waters and ample shaded campsites are indeed welcome.

Even if you lack time to penetrate any deeper into the Crags, this 4-mile jaunt from Cathedral Rock is recommended for 3 fine views along the way. From several vantage points you've a sweeping vista south of Wilson Creek's Canyon plunging in diminishing perspective from 1,800 feet below the trail, to over 3,000 feet deep 4 miles away beneath the 1,040-foot sheer rock face of Sugarloaf, a granite monolith guarding the canyon's eastern wall. Its forested western side rises even higher into massive rounded slabs of granite.

From a trail fork in a meadow .5 mile from Welcome Lake you'll see Fishfin Ridge, a gargantuan granite replica of the spear-shaped armored plates on a *Tyrannosaurus*'s back. From this fork Fishfin may lure you with its optical siren song another mile on the right-hand trail past rockbound Wilson and Harbor Lakes to a notch in the ridge itself. If you're on an overnight trip and you peek over the other side, you're in big trouble: the view of a sweeping U-shaped valley hedged by jagged peaks with Mirror Lake glinting a mile distant and 2,000 feet below is irresistible. You'll be compelled to hike on and explore.

And Welcome Lake itself is no slouch, rimmed by peaks rearing 1,200 feet from its meadowed shoreline. It is a perfect place to regenerate and plan trips to valleys and lakes a scant hour north, south, and west.

From the base of Cathedral Rock the Waterfall Trail drops into a moderate downhill traverse, with frequent view of Wilson Canyon. After .3 mile the downgrade eases to gentle, reaching at 1 mile a small sign high on a tree on the right marking the Clear Creek Trail, which forks left after 2 miles to ascend to Mirror Lake, overall an easier but longer hike than over Fishfin Ridge. Taking Clear Creek's right fork would lead back to Panther Creek.

Bear left at the Clear Creek sign, staying on the main Waterfall Trail, switchbacking down into lodgepole timber, then straight to a rivulet, a good place to fill your canteen. Undulate along a gentle traverse .2 mile in open lodgepoles, then descend moderately .8 mile to another creek that is often dry by August. Climb a short distance over bare rock marked by rock cairns and re-enter woods again until reaching a small meadow at 2.9 miles. Now climb moderately near Wilson Creek and reach a fork at 3.5 miles in another meadow, with the jagged scarp of Fishfin Ridge visible on your right. The right fork leads to Wilson Lake and Fishfin. Bear left across Wilson Creek and switchback moderately for .3 mile, then ease to a gentle climb to another fork and sign at 4.0 miles indicating Welcome Lake straight ahead. The right fork leads to Heart Lake, the left to the South Crags, deadending at Buck Lake. This trail climbs to the 9,000-foot ridge looming over Welcome, and by following it west you've a good opportunity to encounter mountain goats.

Camping areas are plentiful on the east, southeast, and northwest shores of Welcome. Incidentally, its shallow waters precipitate winter-kill of trout, and the lake is usually barren.

Welcome Lake with Fishfin Ridge in the distance

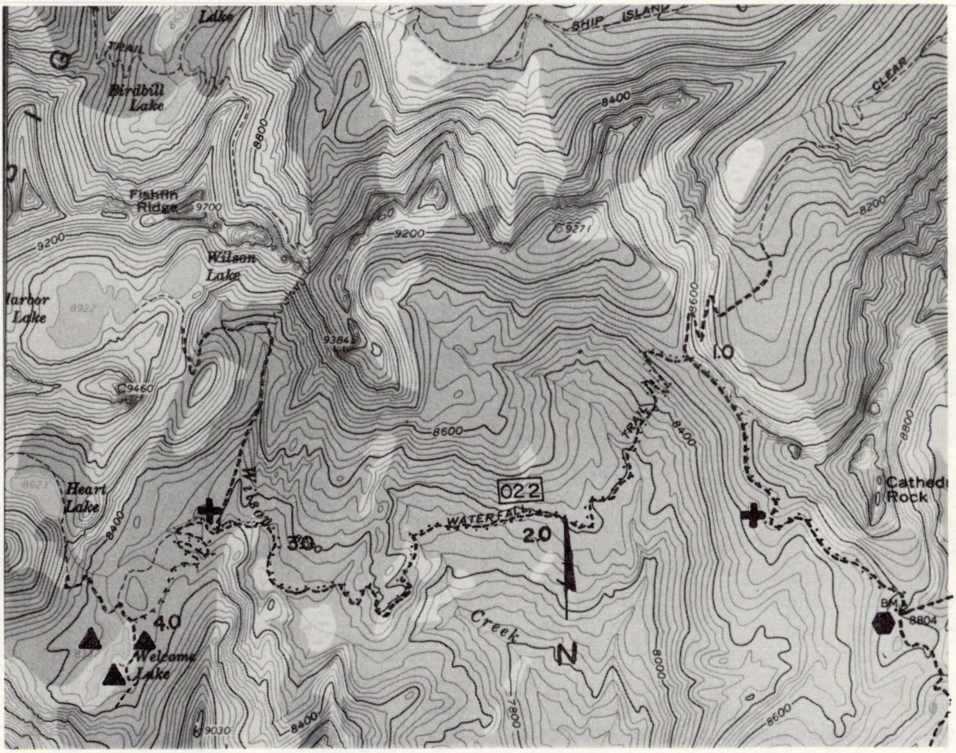

47 BUCK LAKE

Distance: 6.3 miles
Elevation gain: 870 feet; loss: 1,160 feet
High point: 9,080 feet
Allow 3.5 hours
Open July to mid-October
Topographic map:
  U.S.G.S. Hoodoo Meadows
  7.5′ 1962
  U.S.G.S. Mount McGuire
  7.5′ 1962

The Bighorn Crags can be divided into north and south sectors at Welcome Lake according to popularity. The southern area sees fewer visitors, and its western slope draining into the Middle Fork Salmon River offers hiking in trail-less country as lonely as Alaska's Kenai. The peaks are grand, the water cold and clear, and lakes everywhere from which one can procure dinner in finny form.

Follow directions in trail No. 46 to Welcome Lake, and from the fork at 4.0 miles go left to Buck Lake at the sign. Climb in forest at a moderate grade, gradually rising above Welcome. At 1 mile make 6 moderate switchbacks to the ridgetop at 9,000 feet and 1.6 miles. Descend gently along the ridge .2 mile through pines, then veer right traversing the slope's contour. To the south stretches a forested basin that suddenly thrusts up into a jagged ridge about 5 miles distance. Seven lakes are scattered between you and the ridge.

At 2.3 miles switchback left for .3 mile and then right, levelling out in a meadow at 3.6 miles. Hidden in the basin between the 2 concave-shouldered peaks on the right is Skyhigh Lake. Mountain goats inhabit this entire line of crags, and deer seem to be everywhere in the basin. Now enter woods and cross Skyhigh Creek and switchback down to a pond. Wind along the hillside's contour through pines and white soil, cross a creek in a gulley and climb up 60 feet to Reflection Lake. A cliff rises from its wooded shore, and above it an even higher peak peeks. By following Reflection's north inlet you can reach Echo (cutthroats) and Turquoise (California Goldens) Lakes. Reflection, with its limited natural reproduction, offers excellent angling for cutthroats to 14″, but a float tube is advised for fly fishermen plying its shore.

Climb gently for .1 mile along the lake's eastern shore, then veer left and contour around a promontory, up a small grassy swale passing a pond and descend moderately to Fawn Lake on the right. Continue another 200 yards to Doe Lake and then Buck Lake at 6.3 miles. There is no trail beyond Buck Lake, but by contouring south more than 20 lakes can be reached by bushwhacking that show scant sign of human trespass.

Campsites are plentiful on the spit between Buck and Doe Lakes and around Buck's outlet. Though both lakes reportedly hold trout, none were caught in 1977. Twin Cove Lake in a cirque above Doe contains small cutthroats, and Little Lake above it has a few goldens. Both are best reached by ascending Reflection Lake's south inlet.

Reflection Lake,
Buck Lake Trail

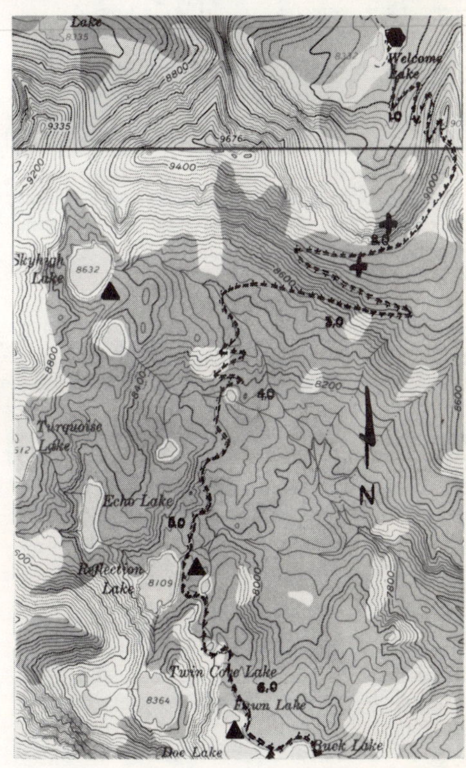

48 TERRACE LAKES

Distance: 3.3 miles
Elevation gain: 700 feet; loss: 600 feet
High point: 9,020 feet
Allow 2 hours
Open July to mid-October
Topographic map:
 U.S.G.S. Mount McGuire
 7.5′ 1962

Hiking from Welcome Lake to Terrace Lakes is usually a shock to Crags visitors who have been lulled by the rolling forested terrain between the car and Welcome. Above Heart Lake the trail had to be literally blasted from solid granite, 3 brave zig-zag etchings across a massive cliff's face that leads to a brutally jagged ridge that plunges 600 feet into a valley with not one Welcome Lake but 4 terraced ones whose outlet cascades into a canyon 5,500 feet deep—3rd deepest on the planet. The view out over the Idaho Primitive Area to the west is both humbling and awe-inspiring.

Rugged cross-country hiking a mere 1.5 miles north or south of Terrace Lakes takes one to lake basins with no sign of human activity. By making a day-trip on the steep trail down Waterfall Creek to the Salmon River's Middle Fork you'll traverse several plant and wildlife zones that pioneer Indian fighter and explorer Colonel Bernard marvelled at as going from snowbanks and mountain goats to rattlesnakes and cactus in 6 miles.

Follow directions in trail No. 46 to Welcome Lake, tend at the sign stating Welcome Lake ¼ mile left turn right and in .2 mile reach a 3-way fork. Ignore the left and right branches and go straight ahead across Wilson Creek and climb gently along a meadow's left edge, then enter woods. Swerve right, make 4 moderate switchbacks and traverse across a cliff's face with a great view of Fishfin Ridge and meet a creek in a defile that in 150 yards takes you to Heart Lake's shore at 1.1 miles. Heart currently has poor cutthroat fishing which will improve when it receives an aerial planting unless the Forest Service's current policy of opposing stocking of high lakes continues. Concerned anglers should write the Secretary of Agriculture in Washington, D.C. Cross the creek and go right climbing moderately in open timber along the lake's right shore for .2 mile, then switchback twice, the lake shrinking below and its heart shape growing more obvious. Traverse moderately to the ridgetop at 1.8 miles. Shutterbugs can get exceptional shots of both Terrace and Heart Lakes from here. Descend left, then right into a .6 mile traverse and switchback moderately down to flat ground at 3.2 miles. The upper lake is to your left, the other 3 downhill right. The lower lakes have the best fishing for rainbows to 10″ but the middle two are sheltered from the wind. It is possible to reach either Harbor or Ship Island Lakes from here by hiking cross-country north. Barking Fox Lake is accessible by contouring southwest from the lower lake, then up its outlet creek to the lake itself. No trout were present in 1977.

Heart Lake from Terrace Lake Trail

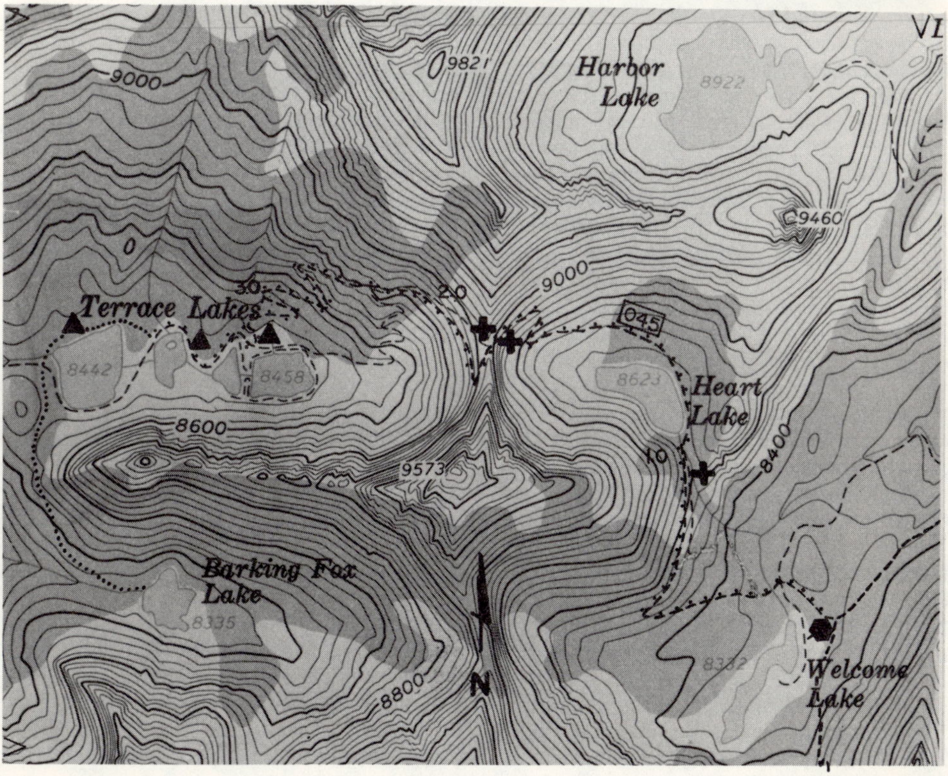

49 SHIP ISLAND LAKE

Distance: 6 miles
Elevation gain: 1,060 feet; loss: 1,540 feet
High point: 9,020 feet
Allow 4 hours
Open July to mid-October
Topographic map:
  U.S.G.S. Mount McGuire
  7.5'   1962

Hiking from Welcome to Ship Island Lake is thrilling because the scale is not only huge but surprising. One climbs between the eerie granite spires of Fishfin Ridge, and as you're gaping at them a turn of the head suddenly confronts you with a narrow valley dropping away a thousand feet to a lake below. Then as you get used to being an ant, a speck as you descend its vast slopes, a quick turn left suddenly takes you into a miniature of the first valley where 4 lakes just barely have enough room. Then when you take a short walk up *its* far side the scale burgeons huge again as you look down on Airplane and Ship Island Lakes in their long bed with 10,000-foot peaks for sides. And far to the west the mountains of the Idaho Primitive Area undulate to the horizon. And if other hikers crowd one on this popular hike there are seven lakes and basins untouched by trails promising solitude.   Follow directions in trail No. 46 to Welcome Lake, and at the trail fork at Wilson Creek obey the sign and go right towards Wilson and Harbor Lakes on a trail that is faint for the first mile. Cross a meadow and then a gulley and climb through woods moderately to steeply for .3 mile towards towering rock pinnacles, cross a level stretch, then up a steep pitch and lose the trail: it angles 45 degrees uphill left, marked by small cairns, then becomes distinct again in 250 yards near a sign stating Harbor Lake left at .8 mile. Climb steeply through a rocky swale, then turn right and make 3 switchbacks over bare granite and

enter woods that lead to Wilson Lake at 1 mile. It's deep, a pot set in solid rock. Descend 30 feet to its shore and at a fork instead of going left to Harbor Lake and its rainbow trout go right along Wilson's south shore, then traverse across the face of cliffs and after 2 switchbacks reach a pass, actually a notch in Fishfin Ridge. A confusingly placed sign states Ship Island Lake 5 miles. Ignore a trail going right and enter a huge, deep valley hemmed by jagged peaks and descend in 4 moderate switchbacks across its head. That lake far below is Mirror. Traverse steeply across the scrub-timbered slope almost a mile, and at 2.9 miles climb very steeply left across rock and descend just as steeply into the narrow trough holding Gentian, Birdsbill, and two other lakes to a sign stating Big Clear Lakes right, Ship Island left.

Undulate across the heather and rock valley and make 5 moderate switchbacks to a ridge at 3.9 miles. The view over the far side is stunning in scale and contrast. On the left 2 parallel concave white granite ridges curve downward and intersect in a spine that plummets to the bright blue, round expanse of Airplane Lake in green forest. To the right 2 gray-rock peaks slope down to the regally elongated length of Ship Island in its sloping V of forest. At its far end a vertical rock dam rises 400 feet.

Descend in 17 gentle switchbacks to a sign at 4.7 miles stating Airplane Lake left ¼ mile, Ship Island right 1 mile. Wind gently .4 mile through woods to a bog, then descend steeply, undulating and twisting to the lake at 6 miles.

Flat campsites abound near the inlet and along the north shore. The lake contains an excellent reproducing population of rainbow, cutthroat, hybrid, and a few golden trout to 2 pounds. To reach Ship Island No. 2 cross the rockslide at the south end and reach in 20 yards a fir with a doglegged trunk 5 inches in diameter where a faint trail begins. Follow it up a creek's left bank for 700 yards and abruptly find yourself in a hanging valley with a large lake whose golden trout have lost the brilliant coloration of their native Sierra brothers. Trout are caught at the north and south ends, especially around logs, while back at the main lake the entire shoreline proves productive.

Birdsbill and Gentian Lakes from Ship Island Trail

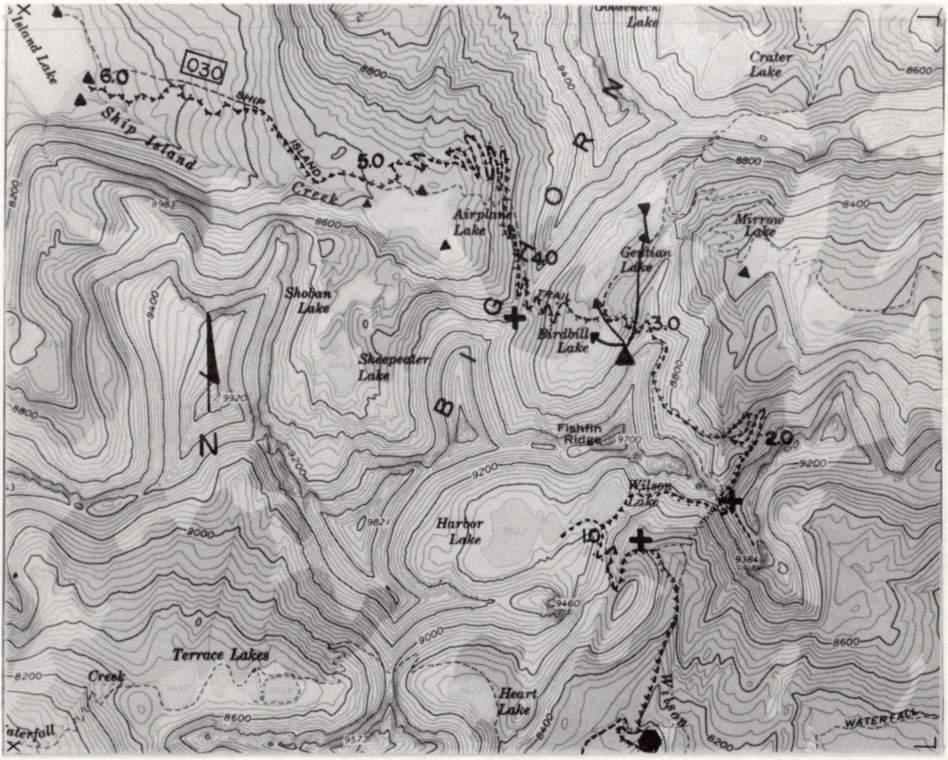

50 BEAR VALLEY LAKES

Distance: 5.6 miles
Elevation gain: 2,300 feet
High point: 9,140 feet
Allow 4 hours
Open July to mid-October
Topographic map:
 U.S.G.S. Lem Peak
 7.5′ 1962

The Lemhi Range rears its fault-block crest to over 12,000 feet from the high desert of the inter-montane valleys of the Rockies that extends from Lost Trail Pass near Salmon to Gallup, New Mexico. Above the Lemhi's sage, cactus and grass lower slopes forests of pine and fir climb to 9,000 feet, where meadows and glacier-carved cirques cradle alpine lakes. Antelope and deer thrive here, elk are scarce,and Rocky Mountain Goats clamber in plentitude along most of the big range's 70-mile crest that is roadless wilderness. The forest had been managed primarily for mining and grazing; consequently hiking trails are delightfully narrow but poorly marked, and campgrounds serve as nice flat grazing and defecation grounds for slope-weary cattle. But the dearth of recreational facilities makes for uncrowded hiking and camping.

The Bear Valley Lakes Trail is included in this book because it is representative of most in the Lemhis, beginning in sagebrush at timber's edge and climbing to verdant alpine country between 9 and 10,000 feet. The scale is huge and it is possible to traverse the range's mostly rubble crest from north to south, dropping off the summits to visit lakes, many of which hold trout.

From Salmon drive south on Idaho 28 approximately 39 miles and 1 mile north of the burg of Lemhi turn right at the Hayden Creek Road sign. Drive about 3.5 miles and turn left at a fork indicating Basin Cr. to the right, following Hayden Creek for 6 miles to another fork and sign directing you right up Bear Valley Creek on road 009. From this fork downstream Hayden Creek offers good rainbow and cutthroat fishing, though most of it is on private land. Drive 2 miles to a fork at Ford Creek and turn sharply right and drive 4 more miles to the road's end at a crude transfer camp.

Walk 60 yards downstream from the camp and turn left, crossing the Bear Valley Creek on a bridge and up a steep pitch to a sign stating Bear Valley Lakes 4 miles. Cross grass and sage for .2 mile and enter timber. You can see 6 miles ahead a high, rocky peak shouldered by forested slopes. The ridge on the right is dry and sparsely timbered with hemlocks, the left ridge steep and densely forested. The creek will flow for 2 miles a few yards away on your left in quaking aspen and Douglas fir, and for another mile provide fair cutthroat fishing.

Climb erratically for .7 mile to the creek's edge in a flat, then climb looping steeply right into a rolling traverse under tall trees shading grass and flowers for 1.5 miles, then veer right across a clearing. Negotiate blow-downs and climb steeply right around a promontory at 2.9 miles. From this rock look south up Buck Creek to an 11,000-foot peak, and .2 mile ahead watch on the left for the trail that forks off left and could lead you to Buck Lakes and its excellent cutthroat fishing in the two largest.

But today keep right very steeply for .1 mile to a dry ridge, dip across a bog, then wind moderately for .4 mile to two grassy clearings from which you climb steeply to a sign and fork at 4.4 miles. Keep left to Bear Valley Lakes, crossing 2 rivulets and a creek at 4.5 miles. Trees block any view. Climb erratically .3 mile to the main creek where a trail forks right to a small lake 1 mile north offering good camping and fishing. To reach more spectacular Bear Valley Lake cross the creek, then 40 yards of bog, then across the creek and away from its left bank. On your right is a meadow, and above a rounded rock ridge enclosing the basin. Climb .2 mile ignoring a fork to the left, skirt a meadow's left edge, up a steep pitch through rose heather, past 3 more meadows and up a final steep pitch to the lake. It is deep, turquoise, lying directly below a pointed peak rising 1,100 feet from the lake.

Camping is best along the northeast shore and in the meadow below out of the wind. Fishing was poor in '77, though a few small trout were seen. Goats were spotted from the lake south into Lem Peak's basin. From the surrounding ridges incredible views along the range's crest can be had for a short climb.

Big Peaks of the High Lemhi's